ED

MASSACHUSETTS

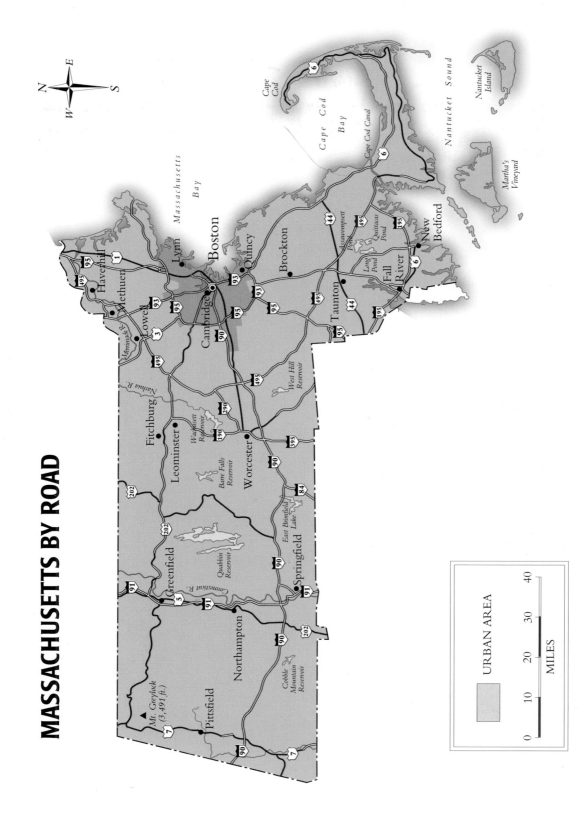

MASSACHUSETTS BY ROAD

CELEBRATE THE STATES
MASSACHUSETTS

Suzanne LeVert

MARSHALL CAVENDISH
NEW YORK

Benchmark Books
Marshall Cavendish Corporation
99 White Plains Road
Tarrytown, New York 10591-9001

Library of Congress Cataloging-in-Publication Data
LeVert, Suzanne.
Massachusetts / Suzanne LeVert.
p.   cm. — (Celebrate the states)
Includes bibliographical references and index.
Summary: An introduction to the geography, history, government, economy, people, achievements,
and landmarks of "The Bay State," Massachusetts.
ISBN 0-7614-0666-2 (lib. bdg.)
1. Massachusetts—Juvenile literature.   [1. Massachusetts.] I. Title. II. Series.
F64.3.L48   2000   974.4—dc21   98-52549   CIP   AC

Maps and graphics supplied by Oxford Cartographers, Oxford, England

Photo Research by Candlepants Incorporated

Cover Photo: Positive Images / Ivan Massar

The photographs in this book are used by permission and through the courtesy of;*The Image Bank* :
Bullaty/Lomeo, 6-7; Steve Dunwell, 15, 60, 109, 113, 114, back cover; Luis Castaneda, 50-51. *Photo
Researchers, Inc.* : Eunice Harris, 10-11, 62; Farley Lewis, 13, 118; Tom & Pat Leeson, 17(top), 121(top);
Robert Zappalorti, 17(bottom); Francois Gohier, 19; Ulrike Welsch, 22, 65; Mathias Oppersdorff, 111;
Leonard Lee Rue, 121(bottom); John M. Burnley, 125; Jerry Howard, 127. *Positive Images* : Jerry Howard, 18,
74, 81; Ivan Massar, 23; Candace Cochrane, 24, 58, 116; David Pratt, 68-69, 98-99; Martin Miller, 73;
Jim Kahnweiler, 84-85, 107; Patricia J. Bruno; 104, 112. *Susan Cole Kelley* : 26, 67, 71, 75, 78, 82, 101, 108,
129, 139. *Gift of Maxim Karolik for the M. And M. Karolik Collection of American Paintings 1815-1865, Museum
of Fine Arts Boston*: 28-29. *Massachusetts Historical Society*: 31.*Corbis* : Bettmann,33, 45, 54, 87, 91, 92, 93,
94, 96, 130(right), 130(left), 132, 133, 134(top), 135; UPI, 89, 95, 131, 134(lower); James L. Amos,136;
Jonathan Blair, 97.*The Harry T. Peters Collection, Museum of the City of New York*: 37. *Gift of Joseph W., William
B., and Edward H.R. Revere, Museum of Fine Arts Boston*: 39. *Delaware Art Museum, Howard Pyle Collection*: 40.
The Bostonian Society/ Old State House: 44. *State Library of Massachusetts*: 47. *The John Fitzgerald Kennedy
Library / © Dorothy Wilder* : 56. *National Portrait Gallery, Smithsonian Institution/Art Resource NY*: 91.

Printed in Italy

3   5   6   4

CONTENTS

MASSSACHUSETTS IS...

Massachusetts is the cradle of liberty.

"Behold [Massachusetts], and judge for yourselves. There is her history; the world knows it by heart. The past, at least, is secure. There is Boston, and Concord, and Lexington, and Bunker Hill; and there they will remain forever. The bones of her sons, fallen in the great struggle for Independence, now lie mingled with the soil of every state from New England to Georgia, and there they will lie forever."   —Daniel Webster, eighteenth-century statesman

"[Massachusetts] was the first in the war of Independence, first to break the chains of her slaves; first to make the black man equal before the law; first to admit colored children to her common school."   —Frederick Douglass, antislavery activist

Massachusetts is home to a singular—and stubborn—population.

"Only Bostonians can understand Bostonians."

—Henry Adams, historian

"You can always tell a Yankee, but you can't tell him much."

—Eric Knight, author

Massachusetts is home to Boston, a unique capital city.

"Boston is a state of mind."   —Mark Twain, author

"The love of learning, learning how to learn—was revealed to me in Boston." —Leonard Bernstein, composer

"I played before the greatest fans in baseball, the Boston fans." —Ted Williams, baseball player

Massachusetts is filled with promise for the future.

"This city is like 350 years of history with a future." —James Koch, Boston entrepreneur, 1994

The birthplace of America, the high-tech capital of the East, the home of the Red Sox and the Bruins—Massachusetts has a history, a landscape, and a spirit all its own. In the pages that follow, you'll learn how the past meets the future in Boston, you'll see where the power of the sea meets the granite shore to create the stark landscape of Cape Ann, and you'll meet some of the people who make up the state's diverse, hardworking citizenry. Indeed, Massachusetts has much to boast about as it enters the twenty-first century. Read on!

1
A PARADISE BY THE BAY

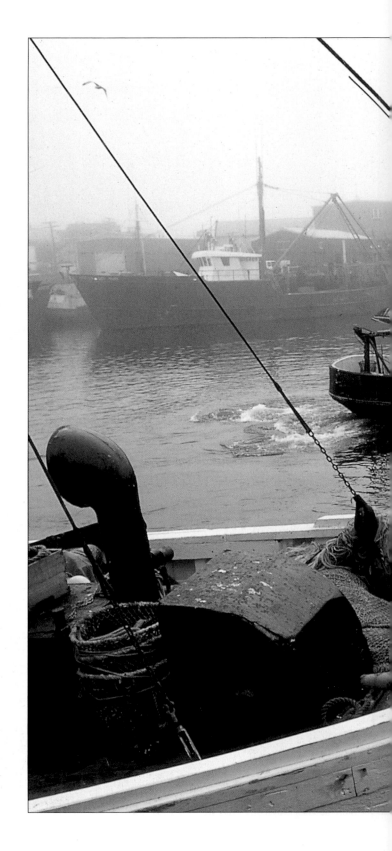

The Bay State of Massachusetts earned its nickname because of the many picturesque bays along its eastern shore. Part of New England, it lies in the northeastern corner of the United States. Every other New England state but Maine borders Massachusetts: Vermont and New Hampshire on the north, and Rhode Island and Connecticut to the south. New York, which is not part of New England, forms the state's western border.

Massachusetts is a small state. In fact, seventy states the size of Massachusetts could fit inside the country's largest state of Alaska. But what Massachusetts lacks in size, it makes up for with its great variety of landscapes. While 60 percent of Massachusetts is forested, the state also boasts snow-peaked mountains, sand dunes, and rocky shorelines.

RIVERS, VALLEYS, AND SEASHORES

The seacoast forms an essential part of Massachusetts's landscape. Beaches and sand dunes line the Massachusetts Bay and the fishhook-like peninsula known as Cape Cod, which sticks out into the Atlantic Ocean. On one side of the peninsula is Cape Cod Bay and on the other is Nantucket Sound, which harbors Martha's Vineyard and Nantucket Island. These two islands offer windswept

The windswept dunes of Cape Cod

beaches and quaint villages to thousands of year-round residents and hundreds of thousands of tourists every summer.

The Massachusetts coastline measures 192 miles from its northern boundary at New Hampshire to its southern border at Rhode Island. But if the coastline of each bay and inlet were added to the total, the state's coastline would measure 1,900 miles—more than that of California. This coast is extremely varied. "I

THE CREATION OF THE ISLANDS: A WAMPANOAG MYTH

According to the Wampanoag Indians, Martha's Vineyard and Nantucket Island were created by a great giant named Moshop. Moshop was so big that he used the whole length of beach at Cape Cod as a bed. Because strange visions came to Moshop in his dreams, he tossed and turned as he slept. One night, his restless movements filled his moccasins with sand, making them heavy. Half asleep, he kicked one moccasin a short distance into the sea. Then he kicked the other farther out toward the horizon. The first moccasin became the island of Noepe—Martha's Vineyard—and the second became the island of Natockete, or Nantucket.

spend as many summer weekends as possible on Cape Ann to the north of Boston, while friends of mine would rather stay in Cape Cod to the south," remarks Roz Kramer, a Boston resident who prefers the north's rocky shoreline to the south's long stretches of sandy seashore.

Some of the state's largest rivers, including the Merrimack, the Mystic, and the Charles, flow east into the bays. These rivers helped make harbor cities such as Boston, Gloucester, Weymouth, New Bedford, and Fall River important fishing and transportation centers.

Central Massachusetts features fertile valleys dotted with marigolds and azaleas. Birch, pine, and beech trees fill the forests. Within this area is Worcester, a commercial city that once used the rushing Blackstone River to power its many textile mills and other industries. The little town of Webster features a lake with the longest name in the world: Lake Chargoggagoggmanchaugagoggchaubunagungmaug, which means, "You fish your side of the lake. I fish my side. Nobody fishes in the middle." "We just call it Lake Webster, it's other name," remarks a resident, with a grin. "It's easier that way, don't you think?"

The Connecticut River, the state's longest river, runs north to south through the center of the state. The rolling hills and valleys near the river are speckled with delicate violets and other wild-flowers every spring. The deep, reddish brown soil here is rich and

Central Massachusetts is filled with beautiful farms such as this one in Lunenberg.

fertile, making this the state's most important agricultural region. Farmers in the valley grow fruit and corn and raise livestock. "I love driving through this area," a salesman from Boston remarks, "especially in the summer when the crops are growing and the cornstalks are so tall. You're really in the middle of the country, but yet you're less than a hundred miles from Boston."

West of this region, the land gets increasingly hilly. The Berkshire Hills is a landscape of high peaks, lush valleys, and cool mountain streams. This region includes Mount Greylock, which at 3,491 feet is the highest spot in Massachusetts.

WHERE THE WILD THINGS ARE

Massachusetts's forests are filled with foxes, muskrats, porcupines, rabbits, chipmunks, squirrels, raccoons, and skunks. The meadow mouse is the state's most common animal. Many beavers live in streams in the Berkshires, while poisonous snakes such as copperheads and timber rattlesnakes slither through the woods. Overhead you can see cardinals, bald eagles, owls, and plenty of chickadees, the state bird. Seagulls fly across the coast by the thousands. "Williamstown, in the Berkshires, is one of my favorite places to vacation," remarks a California native who spends every September in New England. "There is such a variety of species of wildlife, and the landscape is so inviting, especially in the fall when the leaves change."

The state's lakes and ponds are filled with bass, pickerel, trout, and white and yellow perch. In the coastal waters are clams, oysters, lobsters, shrimp, crabs, and many varieties of fish: haddock, flounder, tuna, and herring. You can also find some cod, a fish that used

These North American porcupines, happily eating their favorite food, tree bark, defend themselves by striking attackers with their sharp, yellowish white quills.

Copperheads are a kind of snake with beautiful markings. Beware, though! Their bite carries a strong poison.

The seagull is a common sight along the Massachusetts coast.

to be found in great abundance. A wooden carving of the fish, called the Sacred Cod, hangs in the Massachusetts Statehouse today in honor of the bounty that drew settlers there by the thousands.

Some of Massachusetts's feathered and furry friends have become endangered or even extinct. At least seven species that once thrived in Massachusetts, including the eastern elk and the passenger pigeon, are no longer found anywhere in the world. More than seventy other species no longer live in Massachusetts, including the lynx and the eastern gray wolf. The state does, however, host a significant population of endangered birds, including the roseate

THE RIGHT WHALE

If you've ever seen one, you know that few creatures are as magnificent as the whale. Highly intelligent, graceful despite their size, and almost friendly in the way they often travel alongside ships at sea, whales have long fascinated both scientists and average sea travelers. But some whales, including the right whale, are among the world's endangered species. Current estimates indicate that no more than three hundred northern right whales are left.

Beginning eight hundred years ago and lasting well into the twentieth century, the species was hunted extensively, primarily for its oil and baleen (hornlike plates in the whale's jaw that were used to make serving platters and utensils). The animal's valuable oil, slow swimming speed, and abundance along the coasts combined to make it the "right" whale to kill. So many right whales were slaughtered that its population has not recovered, despite efforts to protect it for more than fifty years.

The remaining northern right whales spend spring and summer off the coast of New England, and late summer and fall in waters off southern Canada. Although the whale is no longer hunted, it continues to face danger from humans: some collide with ships, others get tangled up in fishing gear, and many live in polluted waters. Whale-watching tours from New Bedford, Gloucester, and Boston are popular, but few people see right whales. Only twenty reliable sightings have been reported since 1900:

LAND AND WATER

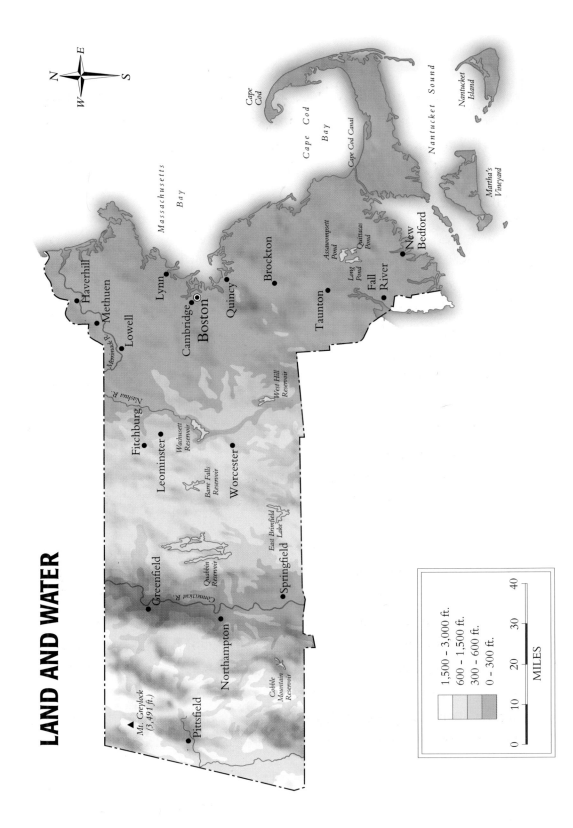

N E W S (compass rose)

Massachusetts Bay

Cape Cod

Cape Cod Bay

Cape Cod Canal

Nantucket Sound

Nantucket Island

Martha's Vineyard

Haverhill

Methuen

Lowell

Merrimack R.

Lynn

Cambridge

Boston

Quincy

Brockton

Assawompsett Pond

Quittacas Pond

Long Pond

Fall River

New Bedford

Taunton

West Hill Reservoir

Nashua R.

Fitchburg

Leominster

Wachusett Reservoir

Barre Falls Reservoir

Worcester

East Brinfield Lake

Greenfield

Quabbin Reservoir

Springfield

Connecticut R.

Northampton

Cobble Mountain Reservoir

Mt. Greylock (3,491 ft.)

Pittsfield

1,500 – 3,000 ft.
600 – 1,500 ft.
300 – 600 ft.
0 – 300 ft.

0   10   20   30   40

MILES

tern and the piping plover. Despite efforts to protect the piping plover, only about five thousand survive today, with just four hundred making their nests in Massachusetts.

THE CHANGING SEASONS

"If you don't like the weather in New England, just wait a few minutes," humorist Ring Lardner once said. Nearly everyone in Massachusetts has borrowed this quote when attempting to describe the state's erratic climate. Like its geography, Massachusetts's weather never fails to offer variety, and lots of it—sun, rain, snow, sleet, hail, thunderstorms, and hurricanes.

Throughout the state, the summers can be hot and humid. Heat waves of ninety degrees and above are not uncommon, especially during August. Thanks to Boston's plentiful lakes and oceanfront, most residents find relief easy to come by. "We hardly ever need an air conditioner," boasts Joan Fitzgerald, a lifelong resident of Rockport. "The breeze from the ocean, along with a few well placed fans, is all we need."

People from all over the country—indeed the world—flock to Massachusetts to experience the crisp fall days and colorful foliage. October is particularly spectacular, with its clear blue skies, moderate temperatures, and splashes of red, orange, and yellow leaves.

Winter, though, is a different story. The winters are long, usually lasting from November to April, sometimes even later. Temperatures average about thirty-one degrees—just cold enough for snow. The average snowfall is fifty-five to seventy-five inches a year in western Massachusetts, tapering off in the eastern sections of the state. In

"There's nothing like a small New England town after a snowstorm," claims a resident of Andover. "It looks as if everything has been covered with icy-cold frosting."

1978, an infamous blizzard broke all-time snowfall records, dropping four feet of snow during one thirty-two-hour storm.

New Englanders must be on the alert for the more than thirty nor'easters that track up the Atlantic seaboard from December through March every year. Nor'easters are similar to hurricanes, but tend to last longer. "The big nor'easter of 1978 was nothing like I'd ever seen," remarks one resident of Cape Ann. "The snow piled up faster than you can imagine and the wind was so cold. But it was the power of the sea, churned up by the wind, that was most amazing. Slabs of granite two thousand pounds heavy were thrown by the waves. This one storm changed the face of the coastline forever."

KEEPING IT CLEAN

The Blackstone River, which flows from Worcester, Massachusetts, to Providence, Rhode Island, was the first polluted river in America. A

Even in the summer, the weather in Massachusetts can be fickle, with cool breezes sending sunbathers for cover.

A nor'easter can churn up the sea like no other storm.

cotton spinning operation named Slater Mill, the nation's first water-powered textile mill, was the source of that pollution. Throughout the nineteenth century, residents complained that the river was making them ill. So foul was the Blackstone that textile mills had to find other sources of water to wash their wool. Pollution continued to blight this and other waterways throughout the state for another hundred years.

The Clean Water Act, passed by Congress in 1972, changed all of that by setting cleanliness standards and providing funds to help the states clean up their rivers, lakes, and harbors. With federal and state help, the Blackstone is now a source of pride. In 1995, U.S. Secretary of the Interior Bruce Babbitt came to the banks of the Blackstone and declared, "The wonderful story is that this river—the first truly polluted river in America, the cradle of the Industrial Revolution—now becomes the cradle of another opportunity, the cradle of revival and renewal."

One of the most difficult challenges facing Massachusetts has been cleaning up its harbors. Harbors in Gloucester, Salem, and New Bedford were convenient spots to dispose of human and industrial waste. And indeed, more than tea has been dumped in Boston Harbor, the state's largest and perhaps most polluted port.

Around 1950, Boston built two sewage treatment plants, but they weren't big enough to handle all the city's sewage. By the 1970s, more than 500 million gallons of poorly treated wastewater were flowing into the harbor every day. By 1984, harbor fish had become poisonous, and more than 15,000 fishing industry workers had lost their jobs. In response to this problem, state officials upgraded the old treatment plants and built new ones. Today, the water in Boston Harbor is much cleaner. Its beaches are now safe for swimming, and marine life (especially porpoises and seals) is returning. Much work has yet to be done, but these improvements are welcome.

Many Massachusetts citizens now take environmental problems to heart and work together to prevent them. This approach helped save Grazing Field Farm in southern Massachusetts. The family that owned the nine-hundred-acre farm cultivated only fifty acres of it. The rest of it was left in its natural state, populated by birds and

Residents and tourists alike crave the salty, firm flesh of the lobster, which keeps thousands of lobstermen like this one working along the shores of Massachusetts.

other wildlife that lived in its wetlands. When the state planned a highway across the farm, the community gathered together to protest. The battle over the highway—which the citizens won—led Massachusetts to pass the Wetlands Protection Act, which is now model legislation for other states that want to pass similar protection laws. Citizens banding together for change: such a spirit of community has been a mainstay of the state throughout its long and exciting history.

2 THE CITY UPON THE HILL

Smith's Point, Beverly, Massachusetts, by John Frederick Kensett

By the time the first European settlers arrived in New England, humans had occupied the area for more than one hundred centuries. The first arrivals were probably the descendants of migrants from Asia who had crossed the Bering Strait into Alaska and eventually made their way south and eastward.

NATIVE AMERICANS

By about 5000 B.C., some of these people had settled in small communities near what is now Plymouth. They survived by hunting, gathering fruit, and fishing. They lived in relative peace until the Algonquians drove them out in about 2000 B.C. This powerful Indian nation set up permanent villages throughout North America. Several Algonquian tribes settled in Massachusetts, including the Nausets, Nipmucs, Pocomtucs, Wampanoags, and Patuxets. The tribe that gave the state its name, the Massachusetts, which means "near the great hill," lived near present-day Boston, from Salem to Quincy.

Massachusetts's Indians lived in dome-shaped huts called wigwams, built of bark, dry grass, and tree branches. Each family cooked on a fire pit in the wigwam; a hole in the roof served as a chimney to release the smoke. They fished, hunted, and farmed, traveling from place to place by walking or canoeing.

The first people to greet European settlers were members of the Algonquian tribes, including the Nausets, Nipmucs, and Wampanoags.

EUROPEANS EXPLORE

At one time, at least 30,000 Native Americans lived in the Massachusetts area. By the time the Pilgrims arrived in 1620, only about 7,000 remained. The others had died of diseases brought by the earliest European explorers.

Most likely, the first European to sight the Massachusetts coast was John Cabot in 1498, who claimed the land for England. The first Europeans known to go ashore were led by Portuguese sailor Miguel Corte-Real in 1502. According to some historians, Corte-Real and his crew lived with the local Native Americans for at least nine years after being shipwrecked.

By 1602, profit-minded English merchants sent Bartholomew Gosnold to the region in search of sassafras, a tree with a root used for flavoring. Gosnold instead found so many cod swimming in the waters that he named the spot Cape Cod. On the same voyage, he also landed at an island he named Martha's Vineyard after his daughter. Twelve years later, English sea captain John Smith mapped the coastline north of Cape Cod Bay, calling the area New England.

THE PILGRIMS ARRIVE

In the early 1600s, a group of English Protestants wanted to separate from the Church of England. They wanted to practice religion in their own way but were not allowed to do so in England. After reading John Smith's description of the beauty and economic potential of Massachusetts, they decided to start a church in this new land. On September 16, 1620, 102 people seeking religious freedom set sail from Plymouth, England, to America on a ship named the *Mayflower*. After sixty-five stormy days, they landed, exhausted and frightened, at present-day Provincetown. The view of the wilderness from the small ship was quite bleak. One passenger, William Bradford, wrote: "The whole country, full of woods and thickets, represented a wild and savage hue." His wife, Dorothy, was apparently so overcome with dread that she threw herself overboard and drowned.

Nevertheless, the majority of passengers were committed to making a new life in this new land. Before leaving the ship, they drew up a form of self-government they called the Mayflower Compact. This was the first time British colonists saw themselves as a political body with the right to create their own laws and style of government. In December, the group sailed across Cape Cod Bay and settled in Plymouth. According to some accounts, the first steps they took onshore were on Plymouth Rock.

THE FIRST THANKSGIVING

The Pilgrims' first winter in Massachusetts was brutal, and many died of disease. In March 1621, one colonist wrote, "Dies Elizabeth, wife of Mr. Edward Winslow. This month thirteen of our number

"For three days we entertained and feasted," wrote a Pilgrim settler about the first Thanksgiving, "and they [the Indians led by Massasoit] went out and killed five deer, which they brought to the plantation and bestowed on our governor."

die. . . . Of a hundred persons, scarce fifty remain, the living scarce able to bury the dead." The rest might have died also if not for the help given by the Indians. A Patuxet Indian named Squanto taught the Pilgrims more efficient ways to fish, hunt, plant, and cook in their new land.

By the next fall, the colony was self-sufficient, and they observed their first Thanksgiving. For three days the Pilgrims feasted with the Indians, thanking God (and their native neighbors) for delivering them from hunger and hardship. More settlers came to the Plymouth Colony during the years that followed, and by 1640 the colony had eight towns and 25,000 people.

THE PURITANS

While Plymouth Colony was growing, a second English colony had begun in Massachusetts. The members of this colony still belonged to the Church of England, but they wanted to simplify and purify its beliefs and practices. Calling themselves Puritans, these settlers started the Massachusetts Bay Colony in Salem in 1629. Boston, the colony's main town, began in 1630. The Puritans thought that their community would serve as a model for the rest of the world. "We must consider that we shall be a city upon a hill, the eyes of all people upon us," said the colony's leader, John Winthrop.

The Puritan way of life was serious and sometimes quite harsh. They saw human nature as inherently sinful and thought entertainment such as dancing and theater were invitations from the devil. Even the celebration of Christmas was outlawed in Puritan colonies until 1681: "Whosoever shall be found observing any

TRIAL BY FIRE: THE SALEM WITCH HUNT

In 1692, Salem Village was a quiet Puritan community. That is, until strange forces seemed to take over a group of young women. Nine-year-old Elizabeth Parris, daughter of Reverend Samuel Parris, and her eleven-year-old cousin began to have fits of convulsions, claiming that an invisible hand was pinching them, leaving red marks all over their bodies. When Samuel Parris insisted that the children explain their demonic possession, the girls blamed three townswomen of casting spells on them.

The village erupted in panic as Parris and his followers accused most of the town's outcasts of witchcraft. Even the wife of William Phips, the governor of the colony, came under suspicion. A special court in Salem convicted and executed nineteen people as witches. Giles Corey, who had earlier testified against his wife, Martha, was pressed to death with heavy stones when he would not confess. "More weight, more weight," was all Corey could manage to say. In total, 150 people went to jail for witchcraft. Slowly, the Salem colonists returned to their senses, and Governor Phips ended the trials and released all those imprisoned for witchcraft.

such day as Christmas or the like," proclaimed the edict, "shall pay for every such offense five shillings." The Puritans lived by a strict moral code. They had little tolerance for those who believed otherwise, and even less for those who lived otherwise. Though they banned all religions besides their own, the Puritans established political freedom and a form of government that elected representatives as voices of the people—traditions still held dear today.

As the two colonies grew, relations among Indians and colonists became strained. The Indians knew they were slowly being pushed off their land. A Wampanoag leader named King Philip became angry and attempted to drive out the settlers. In 1675 and 1676, he and his warriors fought King Philip's War. But the Indian tribes were no match for the settlers, who had much greater numbers.

In 1691, Plymouth Colony and Massachusetts Bay Colony joined to form Massachusetts Colony, which grew rapidly in the years that followed. By 1750, Massachusetts had 200,000 people.

THE ROAD TO REVOLUTION

By this time, the Massachusetts economy was thriving. It had a robust shipbuilding industry, and its merchants were making a lot of money in overseas trade. They shipped dried fish, corn, salt, and lumber to the West Indies in exchange for cotton, dyes, tobacco, and molasses.

Meanwhile, England engaged in what became known as the French and Indian War. Fighting France over the land of North America, England emerged victorious—but poor—in 1763. England was so desperate for money it began taxing the colonists to raise funds. The first direct tax imposed on the American colonies was the Stamp Act of 1765. This placed a tax on printed materials such as contracts, newspapers, pamphlets, and even playing cards.

Enraged colonists immediately formed a group called the Sons of Liberty to oppose the Stamp Act. They did so not only because they didn't want to pay the tax but also because they had no representatives and no vote in British Parliament. In the eyes of the colonists, no vote meant no tax. They protested, rallying around the slogan, "No taxation without representation."

On December 16, 1773, the Sons of Liberty launched a protest against the British government for imposing a tax on tea. They dressed up as Native Americans and dumped 342 chests of British tea into Boston Harbor. This event, dubbed the Boston Tea Party, outraged the British. They sent troops to blockade Boston Harbor, and they stripped the colonists of their right to appoint judges and juries. Tensions mounted with each passing day. Following the Boston Tea Party, future president John Adams wrote: "Now the die is cast. The people have crossed the river and cut

Massachusetts colonists dressed up as Native Americans threw tea into Boston Harbor to protest the rule of the British government in 1773. This incident marked the beginning of the American Revolution.

ATTUCKS ATTACKS: THE BOSTON MASSACRE

A lone Redcoat stood his post, minding his business, in the early evening of March 5, 1770. But in the minds of Bostonians, he represented the British besiegement of the colonies. The colonists were angry and tired of living under Britain's thumb. The presence of Redcoats felt like a grip around their throats. A small group of men gathered to taunt this lone Redcoat with jeers and snowballs.

The news of the brewing trouble quickly reached British soldiers stationed in nearby barracks. As the soldiers arrived to help their comrade, so did more angry townspeople. One local, Crispus Attucks, rounded up some men who wielded clubs and weapons. Attucks was a powerful man of six feet. Historians say he was probably either an African American or a full-blooded member of the Natick tribe, though his true ethnic background remains in question.

A small squad of British soldiers were ordered to load their muskets but not to fire. Overwhelmed by the snowballs, rocks, and taunts thrown at them, the Redcoats began firing into the crowd anyway. Eleven colonists were hit by bullets, and five died. Among the dead lay Crispus Attucks, the first person to die in America's fight for freedom. A Massachusetts patriot named Samuel Adams dubbed the event the Boston Massacre.

away the bridge. This is the grandest event which has ever yet happened."

As news of the events in Boston spread throughout the colonies, the seeds of revolution were planted. Throughout Massachusetts, people began stockpiling guns and ammunition in case the British

Silversmith by trade, political cartoonist by interest, Paul Revere is best known for his midnight ride to warn patriots in Concord that the Redcoats were approaching.

used force. The citizen soldiers called themselves Minutemen, boasting that they could be ready for action at a minute's notice.

In April 1775, British soldiers, who were called Redcoats because of their bright red uniforms, were spotted heading toward the towns of Lexington and Concord, where colonists had large caches of weapons. That night, Paul Revere took his famous midnight ride to warn the two towns. As a result, by the time the Redcoats arrived, the Minutemen were waiting. In this first battle of the Revolutionary War, Britain lost nearly half of its soldiers, perhaps because their bright red coats made excellent targets.

Although the British managed to drive the patriots from their stronghold on Bunker Hill, this early battle proved that the American War of Independence would be a long and bloody one.

One of the most famous battles of the American Revolution was the Battle of Bunker Hill in June 1775. At this battle, the British again lost nearly half their men. This turn of events boosted the confidence of the colonial soldiers. Less than one year later, colonial troops led by George Washington forced the British out of Boston forever. Battles continued, but finally the British and Americans signed a peace treaty in 1783 and all Redcoats were withdrawn from the colonies. America was now free from British rule.

YANKEE INGENUITY

As the young country grew, so did Massachusetts's shipping and trading business. But soon, tensions again arose between the United States and Britain, and the two went to war. The War of 1812 prevented Massachusetts from buying goods from Europe, which forced the state to make its own products. The state adapted well, and Massachusetts soon led the young nation in manufacturing. The state's "can-do" mentality became known as Yankee ingenuity.

The first half of the nineteenth century was prosperous for Massachusetts. Farming communities sprang up in the Berkshire valleys, while toll roads, canals, and railroads were built along the rivers. In 1814, businessman Francis Cabot Lowell built a cotton mill in the town of Waltham. This mill was the first in the United States to turn raw cotton into finished cloth. After Lowell's death, his partners built an entire city filled with mills on the banks of the Merrimack River and named it Lowell. Companies in Lowell made clothing, furniture, musical instruments, and clipper ships.

As the state's economy grew, poor European immigrants arrived to look for jobs. Between 1846 and 1856, more than one thousand Irish newcomers settled in Boston each month. Though initially discriminated against by Bay Staters of English descent, the Irish eventually gained respect in the political and economic arenas. In the 1880s, John Breen and Hugh O'Brien became the first Irish mayors of Lawrence and Boston respectively. In 1892, Patrick

BREAD AND ROSES

On New Year's Day, 1912, textile workers in Lawrence, Massachusetts, began a strike that shook the very foundations of the Bay State. The Massachusetts legislature had passed a law limiting the working hours of children under age eighteen to fifty-four hours a week. In retaliation, the textile companies cut the hours of all employees to fifty-four hours a week, while also cutting wages. Women were particularly hard hit because their wages were much lower than those of their male coworkers.

Words by James Oppenheim

Music by Martha Coleman

During a march through Lawrence, a group of women carried banners proclaiming BREAD AND ROSES! This demand of women workers for equal pay for equal work, together with special consideration as women, echoed throughout the country.

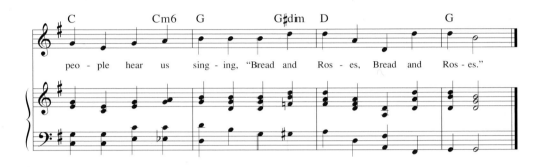

peo - ple hear us sing - ing, "Bread and Ros - es, Bread and Ros - es."

As we come marching, marching, we battle, too, for men,
For they are women's children and we mother them again.
Our lives shall not be sweated from birth until life closes.
Hearts starve as well as bodies:
Give us bread—but give us roses.

As we come marching, marching, unnumbered women dead
Go crying through our singing their ancient song of bread.
Small art and love and beauty their drudging spirit knew.
Yes, it is bread that we fight for,
But we fight for roses, too.

As we come marching, marching, we bring the Greater Days.
The rising of the women means the rising of the race.
No more the drudge and idler—ten that toil where one reposes,
But a sharing of life's glories:
Bread and Roses, Bread and Roses.

The Irish Catholic spirit that still thrives in Boston is embodied in the city's first Irish Catholic mayor, Hugh O'Brien, who was elected to four consecutive terms in the 1880s.

Joseph Kennedy became the first in a long line of Kennedys to hold political office when he was elected to the state senate.

NEW IDEAS

With the arrival of new people of varied backgrounds came new ways of thinking. A new religious movement called Unitarianism developed in Massachusetts. In sharp contrast to Puritanism, Unitarians believed in the ultimate goodness of the human spirit. Many Unitarians practiced social reform, helping to improve working conditions and fighting for higher wages for factory workers.

During this period, Massachusetts citizens also fought for many other social issues. Massachusetts native Horace Mann worked tirelessly to improve the nation's schools, and Dorothea Dix, who lived most of her life in the Bay State, led the fight for the better treatment of the nation's mentally ill. Two Massachusetts-born women, Lucy Stone and Susan B. Anthony, helped establish women's right to vote.

There is little doubt that the newly developed newspaper and book publishing industry in Massachusetts helped spread new ideas, particularly regarding slavery. In 1780, Massachusetts had become the first state to abolish slavery. After that, a strong anti-slavery sentiment developed across the state. This trend spread after 1831, when William Lloyd Garrison began publishing the

"I am earnest. I will not equivocate—I will not excuse—I will not retreat a single inch—and I WILL BE HEARD!" wrote abolitionist William Lloyd Garrison in his Boston newspaper the Liberator *in 1831.*

Liberator, a newspaper that called for an end to slavery. He also founded the American Anti-Slavery Society.

The Civil War broke out between the Southern slaveholding states and the Northern free states in 1861. Massachusetts eventually sent nearly 150,000 men into service for the Union. The North's industries were an important part of the war effort. Massachusetts supplied the Union army with guns, blankets, and tents. The South surrendered in 1865, and slavery was abolished.

INTO THE TWENTIETH CENTURY

After the war, immigrants poured into Massachusetts in search of work in the state's shipbuilding, textile, and shoemaking factories. Many thousands came from Ireland, Italy, Portugal, Germany, and Poland. By 1900 about 30 percent of the population of Massachusetts was foreign born, and by 1920 that figure had risen to 67 percent.

After the United States entered World War I in 1917, factories in Massachusetts manufactured supplies for the U.S. armed forces. But following the war, many industries left the state to find cheaper labor down south. By the time the worldwide economic crisis called the Great Depression hit in 1929, Massachusetts was already in financial trouble. Conditions only worsened during the depression as companies and banks went out of business. In the worst years of the depression, almost half of all workers in Massachusetts were jobless.

Conditions did not improve until the United States entered World War II in 1941. The factories came alive once again, and Massachusetts became a leading producer of war materials.

Immigrants from around the world flocked to Massachusetts during the late nineteenth and early twentieth centuries in search of better jobs. Here, a group of workers begins construction of Boston's subway system.

RACE RELATIONS

Although African Americans had long lived in Massachusetts, their population surged after World War II when tens of thousands migrated from the rural South. Most settled in and around Boston, where they found themselves at the bottom of the social ladder. In many ways, they were segregated, or separated, from white society. Visiting Boston in 1965, civil rights leader Martin Luther King Jr. remarked: "I would be dishonest to say that Boston is Birmingham, or that Massachusetts is Mississippi. But it would be irresponsible of

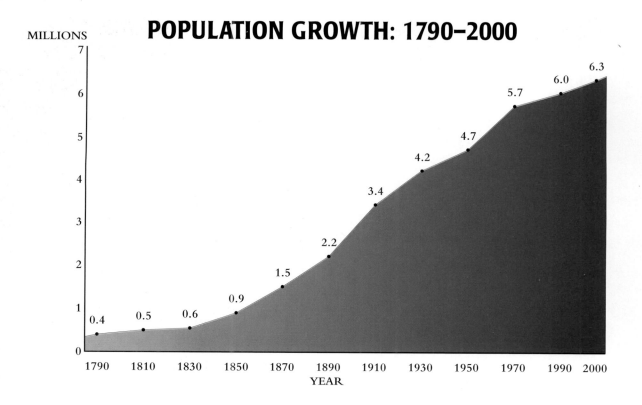

POPULATION GROWTH: 1790–2000

MILLIONS

0.4 0.5 0.6 0.9 1.5 2.2 3.4 4.2 4.7 5.7 6.0 6.3

1790 1810 1830 1850 1870 1890 1910 1930 1950 1970 1990 2000

YEAR

me to deny the crippling poverty and the injustice that exist in some sections of this community. . . . Boston must become a testing ground for the ideals of freedom. . . . This fight is not for the sake of the Negro alone, but rather for the aspirations of America itself."

The government passed laws to encourage integration. In 1957, the state legislature prohibited segregation in public housing. Bay Stater Edward Brooke did what he could to improve race relations. In 1966, he became the first African American to win a seat in the U.S. Senate in almost one hundred years. By 1974, Boston's public schools were ordered to desegregate by busing students from one neighborhood to another, so schools would have a mix of races. But this decision sparked years of turmoil. Even today, race relations remain strained.

MASSACHUSETTS TODAY

In the 1950s and 1960s, the age of computers was dawning in Massachusetts. Scientists at the Massachusetts Institute of Technology and Harvard University played a key role in the explosion of the country's high-technology industries. Research laboratories and high-tech firms sprang up west of Boston, creating thousands of well-paying jobs for Bay Staters. Today, Massachusetts remains a center of the high-tech industry in the eastern United States. It is also a leader in banking, education, insurance, and medical care. Massachusetts's future looks bright as it heads into the new century.

3 MASSACHUSETTS WORKS

The state capitol in Boston

The Massachusetts Constitution was written by John Adams and adopted in 1780 during the American Revolution, seven years before the United States Constitution. It is the oldest state constitution still in use. In fact, Massachusetts is the only one of the original thirteen states to be ruled by its original document. Massachusetts's political life remains almost as vital as it was back in the early days of the Union. "Growing up, all I heard about in my house was politics. It was everyone's pastime," remembers Rita Moan, a lifelong resident of the state. "Learning about how the government really worked— or was supposed to work—made listening to the political arguments all the more fun."

INSIDE GOVERNMENT

As Rita learned, the Massachusetts state constitution divides the government into three branches: executive, judicial, and legislative.

Executive. The head of the executive branch is the governor, who serves a four-year term. He or she appoints department heads and judges and prepares a budget for submission to the legislature. The governor also holds the power of veto, which means he or she can reject a law passed by the legislature.

A lieutenant governor, attorney general, secretary of state, treasurer, auditor, and executive council are also elected for four-year

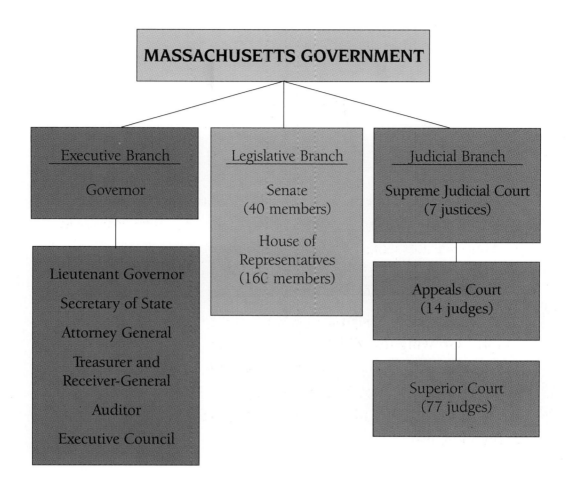

MASSACHUSETTS GOVERNMENT

Executive Branch

Governor

Lieutenant Governor

Secretary of State

Attorney General

Treasurer and
Receiver-General

Auditor

Executive Council

Legislative Branch

Senate
(40 members)

House of
Representatives
(160 members)

Judicial Branch

Supreme Judicial Court
(7 justices)

Appeals Court
(14 judges)

Superior Court
(77 judges)

terms. The executive council, composed of the lieutenant governor and eight persons elected by region, reviews the governor's judicial appointments.

Legislative. The Massachusetts legislature, known as the General Court, consists of a 40-member senate and 160-member house of representatives. Legislators are elected to two-year terms. The General Court votes on bills proposed by its members or by regular citizens. The Massachusetts legislative process is unique in that any citizen can submit a bill to the legislature. A public hearing is held

"The place where man is full-grown," is how Bostonian Oliver Wendell Holmes, one of the country's finest judicial minds, described the United States of America.

for every proposed bill. Two-thirds of the members of both houses must vote yes to pass a bill or overturn the governor's veto.

Judicial. The supreme judicial court is the highest court in the state. Established in 1692, it is the nation's oldest continuously operating court. It consists of a chief justice and six associate justices. Oliver Wendell Holmes, who led the state supreme court from 1899 to 1902 and later served on the U.S. Supreme Court, was one of the nation's greatest judicial minds. Known for his commitment to social justice, he once wrote, "Never take away hope from any human being."

The appeals court, with fourteen judges, is the state's second-highest court. If someone disagrees with a decision in a superior court, the state's main trial court, they can ask the appeals court to review it. Judges are appointed by the governor, but the executive council must consent to the appointments. The judges are allowed to serve until they reach seventy years of age.

TAXACHUSETTS

Taxation provides approximately 75 percent of Massachusetts's income. Income taxes are the largest source of tax revenue, but the state also collects other taxes, including property taxes, motor fuel taxes, and sales taxes. During the 1970s, taxes in Massachusetts soared so high that the state earned the nickname Taxachusetts. Since then, the voters passed Proposition 2½, which radically cut property taxes. "No one likes to pay taxes, and neither do I," admits one Worcester resident. "And I think we could be smarter about where we spend our money—our schools need more help, for one thing, and so many people are without health insurance. But then you look at what does work in the state and how much we've got to be proud of, and you figure it's worth it."

Today, the state's taxes are much lower than they once were, and the trend to cut taxes will likely continue. Perhaps in the near future, the nickname Taxachusetts will be laid to rest once and for all.

BAY STATE POLITICS

Throughout the early nineteenth century, Massachusetts generally supported the Federalist Party and later the Republicans. But immigration changed the face of politics as people of all backgrounds demanded representation. These newcomers tended to vote Democratic. In 1914, Democrat David I. Walsh became the state's first Roman Catholic governor, and during the 1950s, the Democratic Party took hold of the legislature, with a grip it still retains. As is true in much of the country, the state has become more conservative in the 1980s and 1990s. Recent Republican governors William F. Weld and Paul Celluci have concentrated on lowering taxes and minimizing the size of state government.

THE KENNEDY LEGACY

No name looms as large in Massachusetts politics as Kennedy. Wealthy, highly educated, and handsome, this powerful Brookline

Three of Joseph and Rose Kennedy's nine children—John (second from left), Robert (second from right), and Edward (middle)—became U.S. senators.

family was headed by Joseph Patrick Kennedy, an Irish Catholic entrepreneur and diplomat who sent his four sons to Harvard University and instilled in them a sense of duty to public service. The eldest son, Joseph Jr., was killed during World War II, but the other three—John, Robert, and Edward—all served the state and nation as political leaders. While representing Massachusetts in the U.S. Senate, John F. Kennedy was elected president. His assassination in 1963 shocked the nation. His brother, Robert F. Kennedy, was serving as a U.S. senator when he was also assassinated, while campaigning for the Democratic presidential nomination in 1968. The youngest son, Edward, is still a member of the U.S. Senate today. Although marked by scandal and turmoil, the Kennedy family legacy remains strong. "There was a future there," jewelry store clerk Wesley Cwieka of Chicopee recalls. "They did good for the people. We didn't know anything about their private lives, so it was okay."

FIGHTING CRIME

One important issue facing Massachusetts is how best to fight crime. Two of Boston's recent innovations designed to crack down on gang warfare and juvenile crime, Operation Night Light and Operation Cease Fire, have met with great success. These programs focus on putting more police officers on the street and on confiscating guns from the toughest gangs in Boston. In 1997, Boston completed its second year without anyone under seventeen being killed by a firearm—the best record of any American city with a population over 500,000. Police departments in Detroit,

Boston's police department is the oldest in the country, and its officers continue to make the capital city safer for children and adults alike.

New York, and elsewhere have sent officers to Boston to learn more about the project.

MADE IN MASSACHUSETTS

New Englanders have long been known for their strong work ethic. Ralph Waldo Emerson, one of the state's great literary lights, captured this spirit when he wrote, "The reward of a thing well done

is to have done it." Early Bay Staters used a bit of Yankee ingenuity
and lots of hard work to turn their one-man shops into the nation's
first textile factories. Indeed, the modern textile industry began in
1814 in Waltham, when the Boston Manufacturing Company began
processing raw cotton and weaving it into finished cloth all under
one roof. Later, the shoemaking industry also boomed throughout
the state. Paper manufacturers began putting the textile mills' waste
to use in making fine grades of paper, and these manufacturers, along
with rubber producers, became the basis of the state's industry until
World War II.

Today, manufacturing accounts for around one-fifth of the Massachusetts economy. The state's largest area of manufacturing is
machinery, especially computers and office machines. Massachusetts
companies began making personal home computers in the early
1970s. Today, the state remains home to the largest area of high-

GROSS STATE PRODUCT: $223.2 BILLION

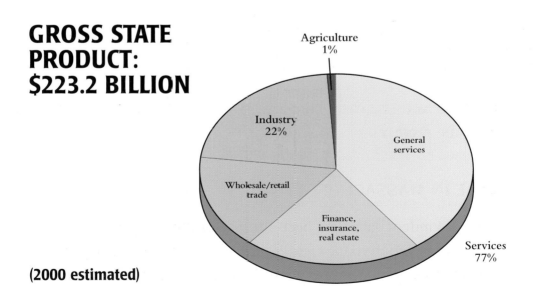

Agriculture 1%

Industry 22%

General services

Wholesale/retail trade

Finance, insurance, real estate

Services 77%

(2000 estimated)

The printing industry is one of the strongest sectors of Massachusetts's manufacturing economy.

tech manufacturing east of the Mississippi River. A host of electrical products, from home appliances to electronic components for aerospace engineering, are also produced in the state.

In 1638, the first printing press in the English colonies was set up in Cambridge, Massachusetts. Since then, Boston has become a major printing and publishing center. Factories also manufacture boxes, paper goods, and greeting cards. Other major industries in Massachusetts include the manufacture of precision

EARNING A LIVING

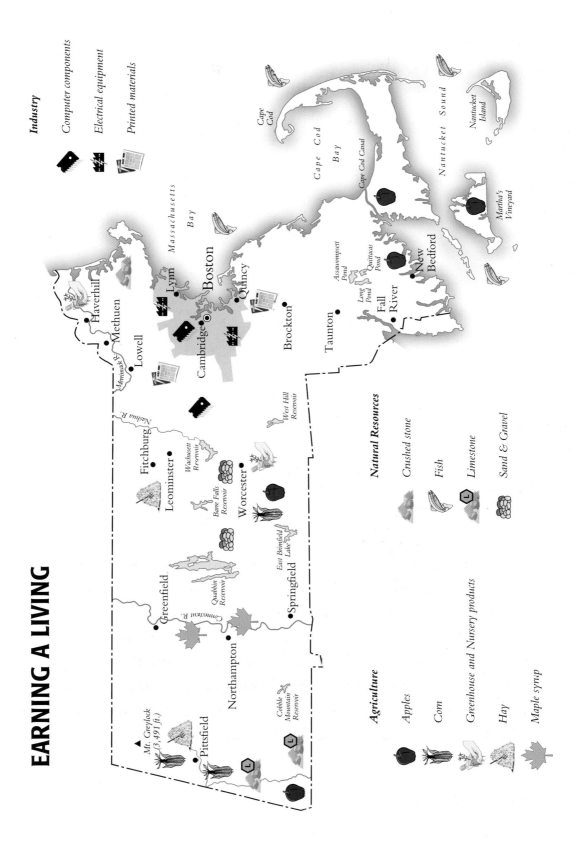

Industry

Computer components

Electrical equipment

Printed materials

Natural Resources

Crushed stone

Fish

Limestone

Sand & Gravel

Agriculture

Apples

Corn

Greenhouse and Nursery products

Hay

Maple syrup

instruments, transportation equipment, fabricated metals, chemicals, plastic goods, wool carpets, and processed foods.

FROM THE LAND AND SEA

Massachusetts is one of the nation's leaders in commercial fishing. When early explorers like John Cabot and Bartholomew Gosnold sailed Massachusetts Bay, they caught so much cod they couldn't transport it all, and they threw most of it back. Today, New

Although the fishing industry fell on hard times in the 1990s, it remains an important part of the state's economy and culture.

TOUGH TIMES ON THE SEA

Sometimes, technology can bring as much harm to an industry as good. This is certainly true when it comes to New England fisheries. In the late 1960s, the U.S. fishing industry began to fall behind as other countries started fishing U.S. waters with huge, technically advanced ships. These floating factories could catch thousands more fish than their small, old-fashioned U.S. counterparts.

The government responded by banning foreign fleets from U.S. waters. It also sank funds into developing high-tech equipment like LORAN, which enables fishermen to track schools of fish. Thanks to such innovations, the Massachusetts fishing industry in the late 1980s had its largest catch since 1945.

But here's the catch—the very technology that allows Massachusetts fishing companies to survive tough competition is slowly killing the industry altogether. With high-tech help, fishermen have gotten too good at their trade. And as fish become scarcer, the industry has responded by creating even better technology to capture the now harder-to-find fish.

The situation has left the fish population of New England severely depleted. Since 1990, the average New England catch has dropped 30 percent. The numbers of halibut and haddock, two Massachusetts staples, have dropped dangerously low. Unfortunately this may be the price paid for what seems to be a case of too much technology. As Fisheries Commission director Vito J. Calomo remarked in 1996, "Man-with-technology versus fish is a whole other thing than man versus fish."

Bedford fishermen provide half the nation's scallop supply, while Gloucester companies catch immense quantities of cod, flounder, haddock, ocean perch, and whiting.

But the state's fishing industry is growing smaller every year, partly because fishing companies are finding it more expensive to operate their fleets. In addition, overfishing has so severely depleted stocks of flounder and other fish that Massachusetts restaurant owners now depend on suppliers in Iceland and Norway for much of the fish they offer customers. "My grandfather fished, so did my father. In fact, when I was growing up, I barely knew anybody who *didn't* make a living on the water," remarks a third-generation fisherman from New Bedford. "But I don't know how long I'll be able to manage to hang on. It gets tougher every year. A whole way of life seems to be dying right before my eyes. I guess I'll have to learn to do something else. I'm sure teaching my kids about other options."

Farming is a small but important part of the state's economy. Half of the nation's cranberries are grown in Cape Cod each year. According to Native American mythology, a dove carried the first cranberry from heaven to earth in its beak, and the cranberry has proven heaven-sent for the state economy for more than two centuries. Today, Massachusetts ranks first in the nation in cranberry production. It is also an important producer of greenhouse plants, maple syrup, sweet corn, and apples.

SERVING THE BAY STATE

The largest segment of the state's economy is service industries, in which workers provide services to other people instead of making a product. Lucrative service industries include hospitals, private schools, law firms, computer programming services, and engineer-

A growing demand for cranberry products has led to an 88 percent increase in cranberry production in Massachusetts during the last twenty years.

ing companies. The computer software industry is among the fastest-growing sectors of the Massachusetts economy. Finance, real estate, and banking are also important service industries. Boston is home to one of the largest U.S. banking companies, BankBoston, and ranks among the nation's most important financial centers.

Tourism is a huge industry in Massachusetts. Approximately 26 million tourists visit Massachusetts each year. They spend millions of dollars annually visiting Boston, Plymouth, and Salem's historic sights and relaxing on Nantucket Island, Martha's Vineyard, and the beaches of Cape Cod and Cape Ann.

AN EDUCATION POWERHOUSE

Education is one of the state's major employers. About one million students attend the more than 1,800 Massachusetts elementary and secondary schools. And Massachusetts's more than 120 colleges and universities have earned it a reputation as one of the finest learning centers in the world.

The Bay State has a long history as a pioneer in education. The first public secondary school in the colonies, Boston Latin, was founded in 1635. The following year, Harvard became the first college, and in 1821 the English High School became the first public high school in the nation. As early as 1642, citizens enacted laws requiring the teaching of reading and writing; by 1647, every town of fifty or more had to establish a school funded by taxes. In 1852, Massachusetts became the first state to declare mandatory school attendance, and two years later the free textbook law went into effect. All children—rich or poor—would be educated.

Today, more than twenty colleges and universities flourish in the Boston area alone. These highly regarded schools include Tufts, Brandeis, Wellesley, Boston University, Boston College, and Northeastern University, the nation's largest private university. Some of the most talented young musicians in the country are drawn to the Boston Conservatory and Berkelee School of Music. Just across the river in Cambridge is the Massachusetts Institute of Technology, a preeminent center of scientific research, and Harvard University, the oldest and most prestigious university in the United States. Among Harvard's graduates are six U.S. presidents and thirty-six Nobel Prize winners. "The worst thing about Harvard," remarked graduating senior Pete Stovall in 1994, "was that college had to end."

The concentration of so many distinguished universities in the Boston area has boosted the state's economy. Research conducted by the universities has led to the development of many new scientific and medical innovations, making Boston one of the most respected medical centers in the world.

Every year, about 7,000 under-graduates and 11,000 graduates attend Harvard University.

4
THE
MELTING POT

Yankee: To people from outside the United States, the word means American. To those who live in the southern United States, the word means a northerner. To those in New England, to be a Yankee means to be a descendant of the original English settlers. No matter who you are, though, if you're a Yankee, that traditionally means that you're stubborn and—dare we say it?—bull-headed. Today, you can be a Yankee in Massachusetts no matter what your ethnic background—as long as you work hard, fight for what you believe in, and are proud of your home state.

MAKING UP MASSACHUSETTS

Massachusetts is a crowded place, filled with people from all walks of life and every corner of the world. Although forty-five states are larger than Massachusetts, only twelve have a bigger population. About half the state's more than six million people live within fifty miles of Boston.

Yankees controlled Massachusetts for the first two hundred years of its history. But by the mid–nineteenth century, a flood of newcomers began to challenge Yankee dominance. In the 1840s, hundreds of thousands of Irish men and women came to Massachusetts in search of work in the new industries. As manufacturing increased, so did the population, steadily bringing in people from

The first American celebration of St. Patrick's Day was in Boston in 1737. For Irish immigrants, it was part of the fight for equal rights.

Canada, Scandinavia, and Germany. During the first half of the twentieth century, large numbers of Italians, Poles, Portuguese, Syrians, and Lebanese also came to Massachusetts. And after World War II, many African Americans left the southern states for Massachusetts in search of work and freedom. Since the 1960s, the number of Puerto Ricans living in the state has also risen dramatically.

Today people of European descent make up nearly 90 percent

ETHNIC MASSACHUSETTS

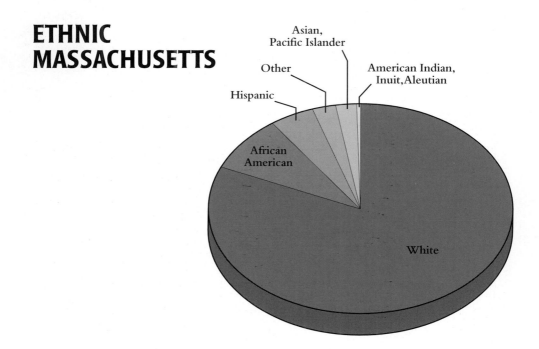

Asian, Pacific Islander

Other

Hispanic

American Indian, Inuit, Aleutian

African American

White

of the population in Massachusetts. Irish Americans still maintain a strong presence in the political, economic, and social arenas in Boston, and the Boston St. Patrick's Day Parade is one of the nation's largest.

The effects of the waves of immigration can be seen in the state's various ethnic enclaves—the Italians of Boston's North End, the Irish of Charlestown and South Boston, the Greeks of Lowell, the Portuguese of Fall River and New Bedford. "Even today, I can walk through the streets of New Bedford and smell the rich aromas of traditional Portuguese cooking," says a Portuguese-born resident of New Bedford. "It always reminds me of home." Each year, New Bedford sponsors the Feast of the Blessed Sacrament, which draws thousands of Portuguese Americans from across the region.

A PORTUGUESE TRADITION IN NEW BEDFORD

For more than eighty years, New Bedford has celebrated the Feast of the Blessed Sacrament, an old Portuguese custom. It comes from the island of Madeira, a Portuguese possession located 390 miles off the coast of Morocco.

In 1915, four Madeiran immigrants initiated the feast in New Bedford, a small city with a large Portuguese population. Until about 1945, the feast had very religious overtones. It was marked by solemn Catholic masses as well as parades and picnics. Although some people today still view the feast as a holy tradition, for others it is a chance to explore the culture of Portugal and Portuguese Americans. Besides music, food, and drink, the feast offers parades, amusement rides for children, and booths that sell arts and crafts. The festival attracts about 300,000 people to the area every year.

About 1 percent of Massachusetts citizens are Native Americans, most of whom live on Cape Cod and Martha's Vineyard. Although few Indians remain in Massachusetts, traces of Native American culture can be heard in the Indian names of many towns and rivers of the region: Swampscott, Nantucket, Natick, the Narragansett River, Tumpum Pond and, of course, the very name Massachusetts.

African Americans make up about 5 percent of Massachusetts's

Children frolicking in sparkling fountains is a common sight during the hot Massachusetts summers.

Even the phone booths have an ethnic flair in Boston's thriving Chinatown.

population. The African-American community is largest in Boston. Despite a reputation of supporting civil rights, the city is not without its racial tension. "I came here from Alabama, expecting the city to be so liberal and welcoming," a black student at Boston University recalls. "But I find Boston is very segregated and I sometimes feel hostility from whites here in a way I didn't back home."

Boston also has a small but vital Asian community, and its Chinatown section thrives with Chinese groceries and restaurants. The city of Lawrence has a substantial Vietnamese population. Many of these people are still struggling to fit into the larger community. "Maybe it would be easier for us if the economy was

A GUIDE TO BETTAH BOSTON ENGLISH

The first thing a Bostonian is asked when outside of Massachusetts is to speak the sentence "Park the car in Harvard Yard," to which he or she will undoubtedly reply: "Pahk the cah in Havahd Yahd." But there is more to the Boston accent than just dropping the letter *r*. Native Bay Staters have more than an accent. They also have a vocabulary all their own. Here's a quick guide to understanding the local dialect:

Pronunciation: In Boston English the *r* typically disappears when it is at the end of a word or when it precedes a consonant in the middle of a word: vigor = vigah; weird = wee-id; corner = cawna. But don't worry, the *r* doesn't totally "disappeah." Bostonians add it to the ends of words that end in an "ah" sound. In this case a word like "idea" sounds like "idear."

Vocabulary: Here are some terms unique to Boston, along with some words whose pronunciation is so unusual that non-natives may not even recognize them:

American chop suey: a popular lunch item made of macaroni, hamburger, and tomato sauce.
Av: an avenue with a long name, Massachusetts Avenue becomes Mass Av or Commonwealth Avenue is Comm Av.
Bubbla: a water fountain.
Candlepins: Boston bowling with skinny pins and small balls.
Cella: basement.
Cuber: the island called Cuba in the rest of the United States.
Foddy: the number after thirty-nine.
No suh!: exclamation for "really" or "I don't believe it."
Tawnic: soda.
The T: the subway.
Wicked: a general intensifier, "wicked bad" or "wicked good."

stronger," remarks a Vietnamese-born citizen who came to the state in 1985. "I think that some people resent us because they think we're taking their jobs. But we just want to live and work and raise our children like they do."

Today, the state's largest group of new immigrants are French Canadians. After English, French is the most frequently spoken language in the state. In recent years, Haitians, Lebanese, and Southeast Asians have also flocked to Massachusetts, helping maintain the state's "melting pot" environment.

THE WORD OF GOD

Though religious freedom was the primary reason for the establishment of the Massachusetts colonies, the Puritans were anything but tolerant when it came to religion. When a woman named Anne Hutchinson dared to question the basic tenets of Puritanism in 1637 she was promptly banished from the Massachusetts Bay Colony.

By the time of the Revolutionary War, other religions had begun to compete with Puritanism. Baptists and Methodists built churches in Boston, and the city's first Roman Catholic church was established in 1788. Mary Baker Eddy spread the Christian Scientist philosophy that the body could be healed through prayer when she founded the Church of Christ, Scientist in Boston in 1879.

Today more than half of Massachusetts's residents are Roman Catholic, making it the second most Catholic state in the country. The other half is mostly Protestant, with the United Church of

Christ and the Episcopalian Church being the largest denominations. A small Jewish community is prominent in the Boston area.

CELEBRATIONS

There's almost always a celebration or festival going on in Massachusetts, no matter what time of year it is. Wintertime festivities include Boston's First Night celebration on New Year's Eve

Bostonians welcome each New Year with First Night, a city-wide celebration of concerts, theatrical performances, and parades.

(complete with ice sculptures and fireworks), the Winter Carnival in Northampton, and the Boston Commons Christmas Festival. In the fall, the town of Plymouth re-creates Thanksgiving, the Head of the Charles Regatta features rowing races on the Charles River, and Harwich holds the Cranberry Harvest Festival. Summertime is marked by the playful Sandcastle Contest on Nantucket Island and the Fishermen's Memorial Service in Gloucester.

The Bay State also proudly commemorates important dates in its history. Evacuation Day, the day the British left Massachusetts, is marked by parades in South Boston on March 17, Patriots Day is observed in Lexington and Concord on the third Monday of April, and the Battle of Bunker Hill is commemorated with a ceremony in Charlestown on June 17.

FUN AND GAMES

On warm summer nights many Bostonians stretch out on the grassy banks of the Charles River to listen to the Boston Pops Orchestra perform at a stage called the Hatch Shell. For years the Boston Pops has charmed audiences with orchestral versions of popular songs by Irving Berlin, Rogers and Hammerstein, and even the Beatles. Free concerts and movie screenings are held at the same outdoor stage all summer long. "I live at the Hatch Shell in the summer," remarks Emerson College student Maria Ameche. "Even as a poor student, I can hear classical music, see my favorite pop bands, and watch movies at sunset without a dollar in my pocket."

The last thing you want to do in Massachusetts is insult the local sports teams; indeed, there's no faster way to inflame the fiery New England ire. Bay State sports fans have enjoyed a long tradition of winning teams. Since basketball was invented in Springfield, Massachusetts, in 1891, Boston has been known for its success on the court. With such great players as Larry Bird and Bill Russell, the Boston Celtics have won an amazing sixteen National Basketball Association championships.

The local baseball, hockey, and football teams have enjoyed similar success. Red Sox fans are ever loyal to the franchise that has fielded a parade of baseball superstars such as Carl Yastrzemski and Jim Rice. The Red Sox play in Fenway Park, where visiting teams fear the park's tall green wall, known as the Green Monster. Although the Red Sox haven't won the World Series since 1918, the fans remain staunchly loyal, especially when it comes to the Red Sox's renowned rivalry with the New York Yankees. "I lived in New York City for six years," claims Jack Green, a Natick resident. "And I never would go to see the Yankees play unless they were playing the Red Sox. It would have been blasphemy!" The Boston Bruins hockey team has produced such superstars as Bobby Orr and Ray Bourque.

Massachusetts's varied terrain helps Bay Staters enjoy a number of outdoor sports. Trout fishing is particularly good in the Berkshires, while saltwater fishing for striped bass, bluefish, and giant tuna off the Atlantic coast is a favorite New England pastime. Hunters flock to Massachusetts for deer, pheasant, and grouse season. In winter, Massachusetts offers plenty of skiing and snowboarding, and when the local lakes and ponds freeze over, it's time to lace up the ice skates. Many residents and tourists spend summers swimming,

Snow and cold don't keep hardy Massachusetts citizens inside. Instead, they bundle up and enjoy outdoor sports like skiing and skating.

tanning, and feasting on lobster at Cape Cod beaches. Crisp fall days are perfect for apple picking and taking in the foliage in western Massachusetts.

Spring brings America's oldest and most famous footrace, the Boston Marathon. First run in 1897, the annual race draws thousands of runners and hundreds of thousands of fans from all over the world. The grueling twenty-six-mile run begins in the

suburb of Hopkinton and ends in Boston's Back Bay. "I placed twenty-sixth . . . when I ran the Boston Marathon," Dan Fusilier recalls. "And even though I didn't win. I count finishing that race as one of my fondest memories. The city was beautiful and the fans lining the streets and clapping made all the runners feel great."

"There is a burgeoning of bustle. . . . The excitement permeates the air," bartender Tommy Leonard says about the annual Boston Marathon. *"The dogwood is bursting on Commonwealth Avenue and it all blends into a beautiful athletic symphony."*

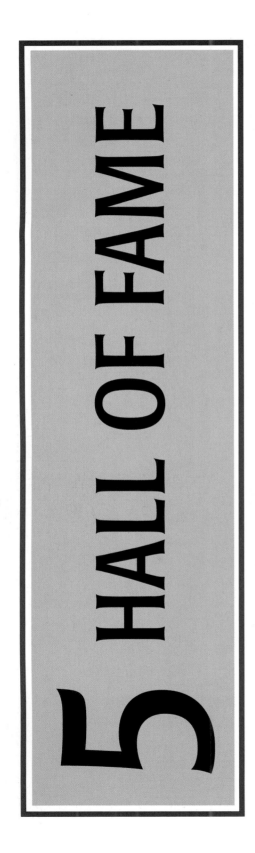

5 HALL OF FAME

"Ideas must work through the brains and the arms of good and brave men, or they are no better than dreams." These are the words of poet and Boston native Ralph Waldo Emerson, and they neatly sum up the character of the Bay State. People with dreams of freedom and the strength to turn such ideas into reality first settled Massachusetts, and Bay Staters remain well known for their tenacity, hard work, and moral character. Let's meet some of the characters that gave this small state such a big name.

FREEDOM FIGHTERS

Massachusetts was home to many early women's rights activists and civil rights leaders. One of the first was Abigail Adams, wife of John Adams, the nation's second president, and mother of John Quincy Adams, the nation's sixth president. Abigail, who was born in Weymouth, was an avid reader of great intelligence and curiosity. These qualities made her the perfect match for a young Harvard law student, John Adams, whom she married in 1764.

John's career demanded much travel, and the couple frequently wrote long letters to one another. Abigail's wit, spirit, and keen intelligence shine through in these letters. She urged her husband to consider women's rights as far back as 1776, when he helped draft the Declaration of Independence. "Remember the ladies," she

A self-educated woman with a passion for politics, Abigail Adams was the wife of one president, the mother of another, and one of the most interesting and powerful first ladies in American history.

wrote him. "Be more generous and favorable to them than your ancestors. Do not put such unlimited power in the hands of the husbands. If particular care and attention is not paid to the ladies, we are determined to foment a rebellion."

The inspiration and guidance Abigail gave her husband often proved invaluable to him. After he was elected president, he wrote to her, "I never wanted your advice and assistance more in my life." One can only wonder about the career Abigail might have had if she had been born today. As it was, she worked behind the scenes with the leading politician of her day—her husband. Abigail died in 1818 and is buried next to John in Quincy.

MASSACHUSETTS FIRSTS

1621: Native American Massasoit helps the Pilgrims celebrate the first Thanksgiving

1631: Boston court officials establish America's first police force

1635: Boston Latin, the first secondary school in the United States, is founded

1640: Stephen Day publishes the *Bay Psalm Book* in Boston, the first book printed in the colonies

1841: Manjiro, a fisherman, becomes the first Japanese to live in the United States when he moves to New Bedford

1846: The first operation using general anesthesia is performed at Boston's Massachusetts General Hospital

1863: The nation's first African-American regiment, the 54th Massachusetts Infantry Regiment, charges Fort Wagner during the Civil War

1872: Dr. Susan Dimock opens the first training school for nurses in Boston

1876: Alexander Graham Bell invents the telephone in Boston

1891: James Naismith invents the game of basketball

1893: Frank Duryea drives the first American gasoline-powered automobile in Springfield

1926: Robert Goddard launches the first liquid-fuel rocket in Auburn

1933: President Franklin Roosevelt appoints Bostonian Frances Perkins as the nation's first woman cabinet member

1944: Howard Aiken heads a Cambridge laboratory that develops the first computer, called the Mark 1

1953: Dr. Joseph E. Murray performs the world's first successful human kidney transplant at Boston's Peter Bent Brigham Hospital

1960: Massachusetts native John F. Kennedy becomes the first Irish Catholic and the youngest person elected president

Perhaps the foremost civil rights activist from the state was W. E. B. Du Bois. Born in Great Barrington in 1868, Du Bois became the first African American to receive a Ph.D. from Harvard. Throughout his distinguished career, he fostered two ideals: equal rights for all and education for all. "Ignorance," Du Bois once wrote, "is a cure for nothing." In 1905, Du Bois founded the Niagara Movement, which later became the National Association for the Advancement of Colored People (NAACP), the leading civil rights organization in the country then and today.

W. E. B. Du Bois was a passionate spokesman for civil rights and equal education for all.

INVENTORS AND BUILDERS

That old Yankee ingenuity has bred some of the world's most important inventors. Born to a Boston family, Ben Franklin later moved to Philadelphia, where, in 1752, an experiment with a kite proved that lightning was a form of electricity. Besides being a talented writer and diplomat, he also invented bifocal glasses and the Franklin stove. Westboro-born Eli Whitney invented the cotton gin in 1793. This machine, which removed the seeds from cotton, helped the United States become the world's leading cotton producer.

Communications took a few giant leaps forward in the mid–nineteenth century, thanks to two inventors in Massachusetts. Samuel Morse, a Boston native, made it possible to communicate quickly over long distances when he invented the telegraph in 1844. Alexander Graham Bell, though born in Scotland in 1847, performed his most important work when he moved to Boston. In 1876, Bell became the first person to send his voice over an electric wire, saying "Watson, I want you," after spilling some acid on his coat. This success prompted him to patent the first telephone.

When taking stock of the country's early innovators, we mustn't neglect Charles Bulfinch, an architect who did much to create the landscape of the great city of Boston. Born in Boston in 1763, Bulfinch graduated from Harvard and then traveled through Europe studying its architecture. Upon his return to Boston, he established an architecture practice in which he attempted to translate English town planning and European architecture into an American setting. Considered America's first professional architect, Bulfinch is

"There never was a good war or a bad peace," wrote patriot, author, and inventor Ben Franklin.

Although Samuel B. Morse had little knowledge of electricity, he figured out how to send messages through electrical wires using a code he invented himself. "What hath God wrought" was the first message sent by Morse code on May 24, 1844.

responsible for much of Boston's architectural character. He designed the gold-domed statehouse, the Beacon Hill Monument, and many elegant mansions in the wealthy Beacon Hill area.

A LONG LITERARY TRADITION

The first English-language book to appear in America was published in Cambridge, Massachusetts, in 1640. Since then Massachusetts writers have provided the world with a rich literary tradition.

Phillis Wheatley was born in Africa, where she was kidnapped and taken to Boston on a slave ship. There, a couple named Wheatley bought her. The Wheatleys saw to it that Phillis received a good edu-

Phillis Wheatley, a former slave, published the first book of poetry by an African American in 1773.

cation, which proved fruitful when a book of hers was published in 1773. It was the first major book of poetry by an African American.

In the nineteenth century, another Massachusetts woman became a great American poet. Emily Dickinson, who was born in 1830 into a wealthy, intellectual family in Amherst, once described herself as "small, like the wren, and my hair is bold like the chestnut burr, and my eyes, like the sherry in the glass that the guest leaves." Such a description is very helpful, for not many people actually saw Emily Dickinson. She spent nearly thirty years almost completely alone, seeing no one but family and a few close friends. Her rather sad, hermitlike existence casts a shadow of mystery over her poetry.

Emily received a more formal education than most women of her

"Hope is the thing with feathers," wrote Emily Dickinson in one of her best-loved poems. Surprisingly, only ten of Dickinson's nearly two thousand poems were published during her lifetime.

time, attending private schools and what would become Mount Holyoke College. During her teens, she was known for her lively wit and sense of fun. But things began to change—perhaps because of a failed love affair—in her early twenties, and she began to withdraw. From 1858 until her death in 1886, Emily spent much of her time huddled over a writing desk in her family home. After she died at age fifty-five, boxes of her witty and poignant poems about love, nature, and God were found, and she became one of America's most cherished poets.

In the 1840s, transcendentalism—a philosophy that insisted that individuals should follow their own conscience—became popular in the United States. Bay State writers Ralph Waldo Emerson and Henry David Thoreau led this movement. Boston-born Emerson explained the philosophy of transcendentalism in his book *Nature*, but it was Thoreau who put Emerson's ideas into practice. His most famous book, *Walden*, recounts his two-year withdrawal from

"I went to the woods because I wished to live deliberately," philosopher and author Henry David Thoreau wrote about his time alone at Walden Pond, "to front only the essential facts of life." Thoreau left his home in Concord for Walden on Independence Day, 1845.

Lowell-born Jack Kerouac had an infectious passion for living as well as a talent for writing: "The only people for me are the mad ones, the ones who are mad to live, mad to talk, mad to be saved . . . the ones who never yawn and say a commonplace thing, but burn, burn, burn like fabulous yellow roman candles exploding like spiders across the sky."

society to the woods near Walden Pond, where he observed nature while contemplating humanity.

Twentieth-century Massachusetts has had its own share of talented writers. Jack Kerouac was born in Lowell and hit the road in 1950. He traveled across the country and recorded his reflections on life and freedom in *On the Road*. This book became the bible of the Beat Generation, a 1950s literary movement concerned with individual freedom and escaping middle-class society.

MUSIC-MINDED

Composer and conductor Leonard Bernstein was born in Lawrence just outside Boston. Bernstein rose to fame as the conductor of the New York Philharmonic Orchestra in the 1960s, but he is most remembered for his scores for the musicals *West Side Story* and *On the Town*.

As anyone who spent the Fourth of July on Boston's Esplanade in

Composer, musician, and advocate for music education and appreciation, Leonard Bernstein is perhaps best known as an inspired and exuberant conductor.

the 1970s and 1980s can tell you, the best-loved musician with Boston roots is Arthur Fiedler. A colorful conductor of the Boston Pops Orchestra for nearly fifty years, Fiedler was born in Boston in 1894 to a musical family. His father, Emanuel Fiedler, played the violin with the Boston Symphony Orchestra (BSO). Arthur eventually joined the BSO himself as a violinist. Bitten by the conducting bug, he organized the Arthur Fiedler Sinfonietta, a small orchestra composed of leading BSO musicians. With the sinfonietta, he inaugurated the legendary Esplanade concerts on

As conductor of the Boston Pops, Arthur Fiedler instituted the tradition of playing Tchaikovsky's 1812 Overture at Boston's annual Fourth of July celebration.

the banks of the Charles River. The first such concerts of their kind in America, they combined classical and popular music in a crowd-pleasing format. The series became a staple in Boston's cultural life and still draws hundreds of thousands of people who come to hear the Boston Pops (under a new conductor) every year.

The list of renowned Massachusetts natives goes on and on. From freedom fighters to writers to performers to entrepreneurs, from the birth of the nation to the coming millennium, Massachusetts citizens have contributed much to the nation and to the world.

6 BAY STATE ROAD TRIP

A trip through Massachusetts is like a trip through time. Preserved landmarks and tributes to a time past serve as vivid reminders of the state's long and fascinating history. This tour will show you a landscape as rich as the state's history, bringing you over rugged mountains, through fertile valleys, bustling cities, and haunted villages, to rocky shorelines and sandy beaches. So fasten your seatbelts, as we explore a state brimming with beauty and tradition.

THE BERKSHIRES

The westernmost part of Massachusetts is by far the state's most mountainous region. In the Berkshires opportunities abound for rock climbing, hiking, fishing, biking, and canoeing. The snowy, sun-kissed mountain resorts lure skiers in the winter. In the summer thousands flock to the Tanglewood Music Festival in Lenox and to dance and theater festivals in Lee, Williamstown, and Stockbridge. "Some of the most enjoyable and stimulating opportunities I've had as an actor have been at the Williamstown Theater Festival," admits James Judy, a New York actor who has performed on Broadway. "And it's so much more beautiful here than in New York!"

The beauty of the fall foliage is best observed along the Mohawk Trail between Greenfield and Williamstown. Some say it offers

When the leaves turn from green to blazing golds, reds, and oranges, autumn has arrived in Massachusetts.

New England foliage at its finest. Today the trail follows sixty-three miles of modern highway, but three hundred years ago it was a footpath carved out by Pocomtuc Indians. Later, pioneers used the trail to reach the Mohawk and Hudson Valleys in present-day New York. Along the trail are dozens of historical markers commemorating Indian battles and the migration of early European pioneers.

CENTRAL MASSACHUSETTS

In the Connecticut River valley town of Amherst, you'll find the life-long residence of Emily Dickinson. Touring her house, you can see the room where she wrote most of her poems. The Pratt Museum of Natural History, located on the campus of Amherst College, houses a fine collection of ancient skeletons, meteorites, and Indian artifacts.

In Worcester, the state's second-largest city, you can visit the Worcester Art Museum, one of the nation's best. Here, you can see

TEN LARGEST CITIES

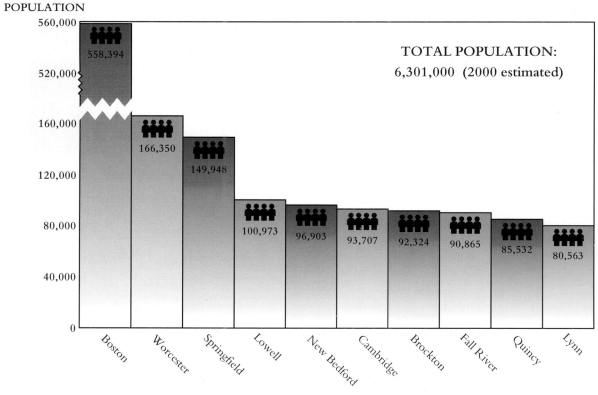

POPULATION

TOTAL POPULATION:
6,301,000 (2000 estimated)

560,000 — 558,394 — Boston
520,000
160,000 — 166,350 — Worcester
149,948 — Springfield
120,000
100,973 — Lowell
96,903 — New Bedford
93,707 — Cambridge
92,324 — Brockton
80,000 — 90,865 — Fall River
85,532 — Quincy
80,563 — Lynn
40,000
0

AND THEN THERE WAS LIGHT: SPOTLIGHT ON GREAT BARRINGTON

You might not find the name of Great Barrington in most American history books, but the little town in western Massachusetts has had a bright past. In 1774, the town was the site of the first open resistance to the British, symbolically lighting the fuse of the American Revolution. That year, 1,500 men gathered around the Great Barrington Courthouse and demanded the end of British rule. Although no shots were fired during their protest, it was a revolutionary moment—they succeeded in driving the British magistrates out of the courthouse. This began a chain reaction throughout the colonies that eventually led to American independence.

Great Barrington's tradition of freedom continued as it supported the antislavery movement. In 1783, Great Barrington hosted a trial in which a slave named Elizabeth Freeman won her freedom in the first case that established slavery as unconstitutional in Massachusetts. Eighty-five years later, the town produced another crucial player in African-American history, W. E. B. Du Bois. Du Bois became a prolific and powerful civil rights activist and leader in the National Association for the Advancement of Colored People.

Perhaps one of the town's "brightest" moments came in 1886, when Great Barrington became the first town in America to be lit by electricity. After townsman William Stanley invented the first electrical transformer, he ran electrical wires along Main Street and connected them to local businesses. He threw the switch and light shone upon a town that had already had many a shining moment.

everything from ancient Egyptian artifacts to paintings by the French master Claude Monet. At the American Antiquarian Society, you can read some of the world's oldest newspapers.

History comes alive in Old Sturbridge Village, where visitors can experience colonial life firsthand with the help of trained guides.

A little southwest of Worcester, you can journey back to a simpler time by visiting Old Sturbridge Village, a re-creation of an 1830s New England village. It features forty restored structures including a school, a tavern, a bank, shops, churches, and homes, as well as a working farm and water-powered mill. The friendly staff wears historically accurate costumes. "I used to take my kids here so they could see what life was like before television and cars," says Ron Parker, a grandfather of four. "But now that they're grown and

PLACES TO SEE

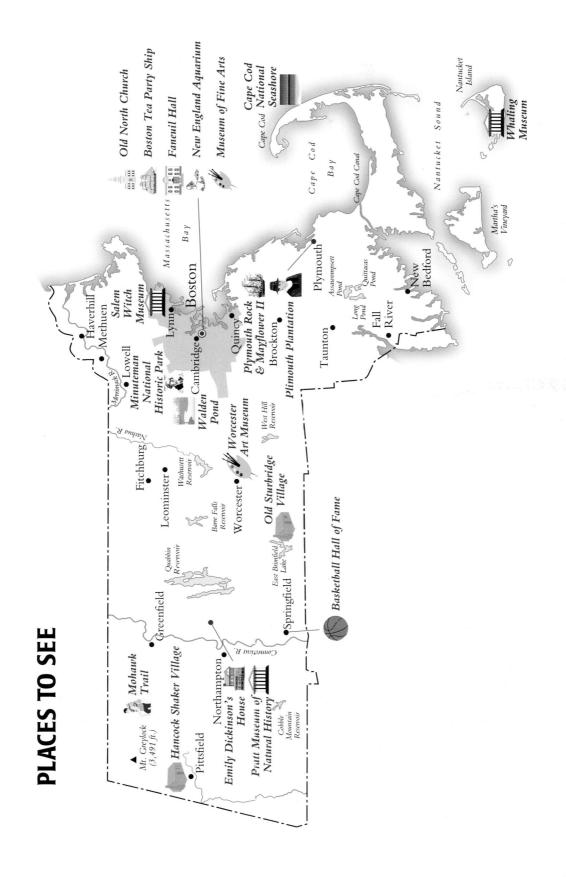

Old North Church
Boston Tea Party Ship
Faneuil Hall
New England Aquarium
Museum of Fine Arts

Cape Cod National Seashore

Cape Cod

Nantucket Island

Whaling Museum

Nantucket Sound

Cape Cod Bay

Cape Cod Canal

Martha's Vineyard

Massachusetts Bay

Haverhill
Methuen

Salem Witch Museum

Lowell

Minuteman National Historic Park

Lynn

Boston

Cambridge

Walden Pond

Quincy

Plymouth Rock & Mayflower II

Brockton

Plimoth Plantation

Plymouth

Assawompsett Pond

Quittacas Pond

New Bedford

Taunton

Long Pond

Fall River

Merrimack R.

Nashua R.

Worcester Art Museum

West Hill Reservoir

Fitchburg

Leominster

Wachusett Reservoir

Barre Falls Reservoir

Worcester

Old Sturbridge Village

Basketball Hall of Fame

Quabbin Reservoir

East Brimfield Lake

Greenfield

Springfield

Connecticut R.

Mohawk Trail

Mt. Greylock (3,491 ft.)

Hancock Shaker Village

Northampton

Emily Dickinson's House

Pratt Museum of Natural History

Cobble Mountain Reservoir

Pittsfield

moved away, I come here about once a year by myself, just for the quiet and simplicity of it all. I can't wait to take my grandkids here."

The state's third-largest city, Springfield, is the sight of the nation's first federal armory, which stored firearms for the patriots during the Revolutionary War. The Springfield Armory National Historic Site displays many weapons that were first developed there. Springfield is also the birthplace of basketball. Sports fans can visit the Basketball Hall of Fame to learn about the history of the sport and its greatest players.

LEXINGTON AND CONCORD

Heading towards Boston, you'll first pass through the history-laden towns of Lexington and Concord, where the American Revolution began in 1775. In Lexington, you can retrace the steps of the Revolution's first skirmish at the Battle Green, visit the Old Belfry that summoned the militia to the green, or have your picture taken in front of the Revolutionary Monument, which was erected in 1799. Down the street, you can stop in at the Museum of Our National Heritage to see exhibits of costumes, furniture, and toys from the Revolutionary period.

In neighboring Concord, a must-see is the Minuteman National Historic Park. Here you can retrace the steps of the British soldiers as they marched into town on April 19, 1775. The fight that erupted launched the American Revolution. Concord was also once home to some of Massachusetts's leading literary figures. Visitors can tour the homes of Ralph Waldo Emerson and Nathaniel

Reminders of the state's crucial role in the Revolutionary War can be found throughout Massachusetts. This statue of a Minuteman stands in Lexington, where the first shot of the American War of Independence was fired.

Historic re-creations help today's men, women, and children better understand how wars were fought in days gone by.

Hawthorne as well as Orchard House, the residence of Louisa May Alcott and the setting for her novel *Little Women*. After taking in all of this history, you can gather your thoughts and find a bit of serenity in the wooded trails of Walden Pond, just as writer-philosopher Henry David Thoreau did in the nineteenth century. You'll find Thoreau's final resting place, as well as those of Emerson, Alcott, and Hawthorne, in the nearby greens of the Sleepy Hollow Cemetery.

THE NORTH SHORE

The North Shore stretches from Boston to Cape Ann. Cape Ann is home to the picturesque towns of Gloucester and Rockport. Gloucester is still a town that lives off the sea. It is the site of the famous Fisherman statue—perhaps better known as the Gorton's Fisherman, because the seafood company uses it on all its packaging—a tribute to all the fishermen who have given their lives at sea.

A popular subject for artists, this red barn in Rockport Harbor is one of the most painted buildings in the United States.

You'll certainly want to break from your tour to enjoy a seafood lunch of the freshest catch in New England before you experience some of the North Shore's cultural attractions. If art is what you crave, you should head over to Rockport, a seaside town chock-full of artists. At the James Babson Cooperage Shop on the outskirts of town you can see displays of early American tools and furniture, while a visit to the Rockport Art Association will familiarize you with the work of local artists. Cape Ann is also an excellent place to join a whale-watching tour, during which you're almost guaranteed to spot one of these great creatures in their natural habitat.

Moving southward from Cape Ann, you might want to stop by the beautiful town of Marblehead to view some well-kept nineteenth-century mansions. However, before it gets too late, you should be sure to reach Salem, the one town you don't want to be alone in after the witching hour! Salem is the site of the infamous Salem witch trials of 1692. The Salem Witch Museum offers visitors a look at one of the most emotional and tragic events of early American history. The town draws more than a million tourists a year who enjoy getting spooked at the Salem Witch Village, the Witch House, and the Witch Dungeon Museum, which features an acclaimed re-creation of a witch trial adapted from actual court transcripts.

BOSTON

Boston, the state's capital and largest city, is worth a trip to Massachusetts just for itself. It is a historic city, a modern metropolis, and a cultural center all in one. There is much to see and more to do. Let's take a closer look.

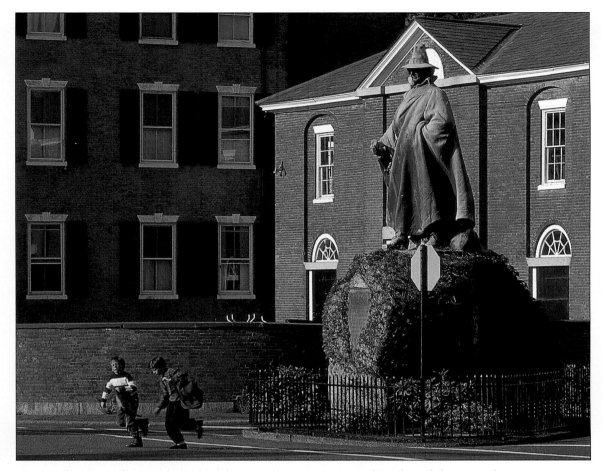

The stern face and cloaked figure of Roger Conant, founder of the city of Salem, recall the harsh moral code of the Puritans who settled in the area during the seventeenth century.

Historic Boston. The Public Garden, located smack-dab in the middle of the city, is a good place to begin your tour. Walkers and bikers fill the paths that cut through the flower-filled garden. The greens are covered with students studying or playing Frisbee. All about are children begging their mothers for a ride on the famous swan boats or a chance to sit on the iron ducklings that are a tribute to the classic children's story *Make Way for Ducklings* by Robert McCloskey.

The Public Garden leads to the Boston Common, the country's oldest park and the beginning of the Freedom Trail, a 2.5-mile walking tour that links fourteen of Boston's most important historic landmarks. Among them are the Park Street Church, where William Lloyd Garrison gave his first antislavery speech; the Old South Meeting House, where the Boston Tea Party was planned; the Paul Revere House; and the Old North Church, where lanterns were hung to warn the colonists of British invasion.

Literature comes to life with these adorable sculptures inspired by the children's book Make Way for Ducklings. *"Every time we came to the park, I had to take my little girls here to play on the ducks," recalls one visitor. "Now I have to take my grandchildren!"*

You can find this memorial to the 54th Massachusetts Infantry Regiment, the first regiment of black soldiers in the Civil War, in the Boston African-American Park.

Also along the trail is one of the city's most popular tourist attractions, Faneuil Hall. Once the meeting hall and market where the patriots of the American Revolution met, it now houses Quincy Market, which includes more than 125 restaurants and shops. The Freedom Trail ends at Bunker Hill, where a monument commemorates the 1775 victory of the patriots over the British.

Another historic walking tour is the African-American Heritage

Trail. A highlight of the tour is the Boston African-American Park. This site includes fifteen pre–Civil War structures relating to the city's African-American community, including the African Meeting House, the oldest standing African-American church in the United States.

An Artful City. Boston's architecture is a remarkable blend of old and new. The sixty-story John Hancock Tower, New England's

Old meets new in Boston's Copley Square. Trinity Church, described by one architect as "the reigning monarch of the richest architectural space in Boston," is reflected in the sparkling glass of a modern skyscraper designed by I. M. Pei.

highest skyscraper, stands right behind Trinity Church, one of Boston's oldest churches. "You can see the reflection of the historic Trinity Church in the windows of the very modern John Hancock skyscraper. You can read about cutting-edge research performed at the Massachusetts Institute of Technology while sitting in the Old North Church. I love the contrasts of this city," remarks Craig Wong, a Boston University student. An elevator ride to the top of the Prudential Center provides breathtaking views of the city and beyond, while a stroll through the cobblestone streets of the Beacon Hill neighborhood takes you to a time gone by.

Boston museums and galleries store the city's wealth of art and antiquities. The Museum of Fine Arts, the Isabella Stewart Gardner Museum, and the Institute of Contemporary Art are just a few of the places in the city to view Renaissance paintings, Egyptian mummies, American folk art, and the latest in modern art and design. Newbury Street, in the city's Back Bay, is lined with small galleries and shops.

At the New England Aquarium, you can see more than two thousand fish and sea animals, pat a sea lion on the head, and visit with a colony of penguins. Located nearby on Museum Wharf, the Children's Museum offers hands-on science exhibits. Also along this wharf is the Boston Tea Party Ship, a floating, full-scale replica of the original ship. Visitors are even allowed to hurl some tea off the side of the ship, just like the patriots did in 1773.

With so many different things to do and see in Boston, leaving the city won't be easy. But no tour of Massachusetts is complete without a visit to the beaches of the South Shore and the islands beyond.

THE SOUTH SHORE AND CAPE COD

The southern arm of Massachusetts Bay, known as the South Shore, is home to Plymouth. It was at Plymouth Rock that the Pilgrims landed in 1620 to found the first permanent European settlement north of Virginia. Today, visitors can view Plymouth Rock and tour a replica of the *Mayflower*. On board, costumed guides portraying passengers describe the difficult journey across the Atlantic. Back on land, the National Monument to the Forefathers bears the names of the 102 *Mayflower* passengers.

Visitors can experience what life was like in the first Pilgrim settlement at Plimouth Plantation.

INDIAN PUDDING

The Pilgrims' first few winters in the New World were rough ones indeed, for food was scarce. One staple they had in abundance, thanks to help from local Native Americans, was corn. These early settlers created this savory dessert using cornmeal as a base. You can make the same dessert yourself, with help from an adult. Just follow these easy directions:

⅓ cup plus 1 tablespoon cornmeal
4 cups whole milk
½ cup molasses
4 tablespoons unsalted butter
2 tablespoons sugar
1½ teaspoons ground ginger
½ teaspoon salt

Preheat oven to 275 degrees. Place the cornmeal in a large saucepan. Stir in the milk very slowly, to avoid lumps. Stirring constantly, bring the mixture to a boil over medium heat and cook for 3 minutes. Reduce the heat as low as possible and cook for 15 minutes, stirring frequently. Remove the dish from heat. Then stir in the remaining ingredients.

Butter a 9-inch baking dish. Pour the mixture into it. Bake until the center looks firm but is still slightly quivery when the dish is shaken—make sure to use oven mitts! A dark crust will form on top. Let cool on a rack for 30 minutes to 1 hour. Then enjoy with a scoop of ice cream or a dollop of fresh whipped cream.

For beachcombers and swimmers, nothing beats the beautiful coast of Cape Cod.

You can step back into seventeenth-century New England at Plimoth Plantation, a living history museum that re-creates the early Pilgrim town. Here you can learn about the hardships the Pilgrims faced by talking to costumed guides as they perform the tasks of everyday life in the colony.

Cape Cod, the peninsula at the southeastern end of Massachusetts, is a favorite summer getaway spot for millions of city dwellers. The Upper Cape, the area closest to the mainland, is speckled with acres of cranberry bogs and small ponds, while the Lower Cape is known for its sand dunes and sunny beaches.

In between the Upper and Lower Capes is Hyannis, best known as the summer resort of the Kennedy family and for the ferries that take passengers to Nantucket Island and Martha's Vineyard. Martha's Vineyard is a popular vacation area that attracts artists and celebrities—including President Bill Clinton—to its pristine beaches. Nantucket's charm is more associated with its cobblestone streets and quaint villages.

At the cape's (and the state's) farthest tip lies Provincetown, where the Pilgrims first landed before they settled in Plymouth. For such a small, isolated community, the town has quite a cosmopolitan mix of people. The beachfront is serene and relaxing, while the only two commercial streets in town are lined with discos, museums, shops, and a wide variety of restaurants. The attitude here is fun, open, and carefree—quite a contrast to the Puritan ethic that once dominated Massachusetts.

THE FLAG: The Massachusetts flag shows the shield that appears on the state seal against a white background.

THE SEAL: In the center of the Massachusetts state seal is a gold Indian on a blue shield. The Indian's arrow is pointing downward, to show that he is peaceful. Above the Indian is a silver star, which indicates that Massachusetts was one of the original 13 states. The arm holding a sword illustrates the state motto, which is written in Latin on the ribbon below the shield.

STATE SURVEY

Statehood: February 6, 1788

Origin of Name: From the Massachusetts, an Indian tribe whose name means "near the great hill."

Nickname: Bay State

Capital: Boston

Motto: By the Sword We Seek Peace, but Peace Only under Liberty

Bird: Chickadee

Flower: Mayflower

Tree: American elm

Fish: Cod

Beverage: Cranberry juice

Chickadee

Mayflower

MASSACHUSETTS

Arlo Guthrie composed this song in 1976. Massachusetts is the only state to have a song designated as the official state folk song.

Words and Music by Arlo Guthrie

The sun comes up to meet the dawn, another day that must go on,
There's another night that's gone in Massachusetts.
And I could spend all of my days, and remain each day amazed
At the way each day is phrased in Massachusetts. *Chorus*

Now if you could only see, well I know you would agree,
There ain't nowhere else to be like Massachusetts.
And there's a house upon a hill that keeps us from the chill,
And by the Grace of God we will be in Massachusetts. *Chorus*

Dog: Boston terrier

Horse: Morgan

Insect: Ladybug

Marine Mammal: Right whale

Mineral: Babingtonite

Stone: Granite

Dessert: Boston creme pie

GEOGRAPHY

Highest Point: 3,491 feet above sea level, at Mount Greylock

Lowest Point: sea level, along the Atlantic coast

Area: 8,262 square miles

Greatest Distance, North to South: 113 miles

Greatest Distance, East to West: 183 miles

Bordering States: Vermont and New Hampshire to the north; New York to the west; Connecticut and Rhode Island to the south

Hottest Recorded Temperature: 107°F in New Bedford and Chester on August 2, 1975

Coldest Recorded Temperature: -34°F at Birch Hill Dam on January 18, 1957

Average Annual Precipitation: 45 inches

Major Rivers: Blackstone, Charles, Chicopee, Concord, Connecticut, Deerfield, Hoosic, Housatonic, Merrimack, Millers, Mystic, Nashua, Neponset, Westfield

Major Lakes: Assawompsett, Long Pond, North Watuppa, Quabbin, Wachusett, Webster

Trees: ash, beech, birch, eastern hemlock, eastern white pine, maple, oak, pitch pine, red pine

Wild Plants: azalea, dogwood, marigold, mountain laurel, skunk cabbage, rhododendron, rush, sedge, trillium, viburnum, violet

Animals: beaver, copperhead snake, deer, fox, meadow mouse, muskrat, porcupine, rabbit, raccoon, right whale, skunk, timber rattlesnake

Birds: eastern meadowlark, grebe, hawk, heron, partridge, pheasant, pileated woodpecker, purple martin, robin, sparrow, tern, warbler, wild turkey

Fish: bass, cod, flounder, haddock, pickerel, sunfish, swordfish, trout, tuna, white perch, whiting, yellow perch

Bog turtle

Endangered Animals: American burying beetle, American peregrine falcon, bald eagle, bog turtle, dwarf wedgemussel, northeastern beach tiger beetle, piping plover, Plymouth red-belly turtle, Puritan tiger beetle, roseate tern

Endangered Plants: northeastern bulrush, sandplain gerardia, small whorled pogonia

TIMELINE

Massachusetts History

1500s Nauset, Nipmuc, Patuxet, Pocomtuc, and Wampanoag Indians live in the area

1602 Bartholomew Gosnold becomes the first European known to land in present-day Massachusetts

1620 The Pilgrims arrive at Plymouth

1629 The Puritans found Massachusetts Bay Colony

1630 Boston is founded

1635 Boston Latin School, the first secondary school in the American colonies, is established

1636 Harvard, the first college in the American colonies, is founded

1640 The *Bay Psalm Book*, America's first English-language book, is published in Cambridge

1676 Colonists defeat the Wampanoag Indians in King Philip's War

1690 The American colonies' first newspaper, *Publick Occurrences Both Forreign and Domestick*, is established in Boston

1692 Nineteen people are executed during the Salem witch hunts

1770 British soldiers kill five colonists in the Boston Massacre

1773 Colonists dump British tea into Boston Harbor during the Boston Tea Party

1775 The American Revolution begins at the Battle of Lexington and Concord

1780 The Massachusetts Constitution is adopted

1788 Massachusetts becomes the sixth state

1796 Bay Stater John Adams is elected the nation's second president

1814 Francis Cabot Lowell opens a mill in Waltham where all the stages of cloth manufacturing take place, marking the beginning of the U.S. textile industry

1824 Bay Stater John Quincy Adams is elected the sixth president

1831 William Lloyd Garrison begins publishing his antislavery newspaper, the *Liberator* in Boston

1837 Mount Holyoke, the nation's first women's college, is established in South Hadley

1852 Massachusetts becomes the first state in the Union to require children to attend school

1861–1865 About 150,000 Bay Staters serve in the Union army during the Civil War

1876 Alexander Graham Bell invents the telephone in Boston

1897 The nation's first subway begins operation in Boston

1903 Baseball's first World Series is played in Boston

1939–1945 World War II

1960 Massachusetts native John F. Kennedy is elected president

1974 Boston begins busing to desegregate schools

1980 Massachusetts voters pass Proposition 2½, which drastically cuts property taxes

1988 Massachusetts celebrates its 200th anniversary as a state

ECONOMY

Agricultural Products: apples, cranberries, eggs, greenhouse plants, maple syrup, milk, sweet corn

Manufactured Products: computer components, electrical equipment, metals, printed materials, processed foods, scientific instruments, transportation equipment

Apples

Natural Resources: crushed stone, fish, granite, marble, sand and gravel

Business and Trade: banking, education, medical care, real estate, research, tourism, wholesale and retail trade

CALENDAR OF CELEBRATIONS

Chinese New Year Boston marks the beginning of the Chinese calendar in January or February with lots of exploding firecrackers and a parade featuring long dancing serpents.

St. Patrick's Day Everyone's Irish on March 17, when Boston holds one of the nation's largest St. Patrick's Day parades.

Patriots Day Everyone in Lexington is up early on this April morning when the beginning of the American Revolution is reenacted. At 6 A.M., a man dressed as Paul Revere begins the festivities by galloping through town shouting, "The British are coming!"

World's Largest Pancake Breakfast In just three hours one May morning in Springfield, 60,000 people sit down at a four-block-long table to eat their fill of pancakes served up by 400 volunteers.

Tanglewood For more than two months beginning in late June, Lenox hosts one of the world's premiere classical music festivals. Hundreds of thousands of people enjoy symphonies, choral music, jazz, and more in the beautiful Berkshire Hills.

Boston Harborfest More than a million people attend six days worth of events in Boston in late June and early July. Highlights include a jazz concert, a fleet of tall ships sailing into Boston Harbor, a contest for the best New England clam chowder, and a spectacular Fourth of July fireworks display.

Boston Harborfest

Lowell Folk Festival At this July festival in Lowell, you might hear music ranging from Eskimo singers to Vietnamese bands. In addition to all the music, you can attend parades, dances, and international craft demonstrations.

Caribbean Carnival The highlight of this August event in Boston is a parade filled with colorful costumes, elaborate floats, and huge steel drum groups. You can also taste spicy Caribbean food.

Essex ClamFest Essex claims to have invented fried clams in 1916. Each September, the town honors its clam history at an event where you can eat clams fried or in fritters, cakes, or chowder. Apart from the food, pony rides, Dixieland jazz bands, and arts exhibits keep everyone happy.

Cranberry Harvest Festival Each September 200,000 people descend on Harwich to honor Massachusetts's most famous agricultural product. You can savor cranberry drinks, breads, muffins, and jellies while watching a parade.

Head of the Charles Regatta Boston hosts one of the world's largest rowing events each October. More than 4,500 rowers compete in events on the Charles River.

Thanksgiving Day On Thanksgiving day in November, feasts are held throughout Plymouth, the site of the first Thanksgiving. A parade, complete with marching bands and floats, tops off the festivities.

First Night On the last day of December, Boston celebrates the new year with music, dance, mimes, ice sculptures, children's activities, and fireworks.

John Adams

STATE STARS

John Adams (1735–1826), of Braintree, was the second president of the United States. Before the American Revolution, Adams argued for independence when many colonial leaders were still trying to settle their differences with Britain. As a member of the Continental Congress, he pushed for the adoption of the Declaration of Independence. He also drafted the Massachusetts Constitution. His son John Quincy Adams was the nation's sixth president.

Louisa May Alcott (1832–1888) wrote the classic novel *Little Women*. This story of four sisters growing up in New England was based on her own life. Besides writing other classic family novels such as *Little Men* and *Jo's Boys*, she also wrote thrillers under a fake name in order to earn money. Alcott grew up in Boston.

Crispus Attucks (1723?–1770), the first person killed in the American colonies' fight for

Louisa May Alcott

freedom, died during the Boston Massacre. Little is known of Attucks's background, but many historians believe he was African American.

Clara Barton (1821–1912) founded the American Red Cross and served as its president for more than 20 years. Barton, who was born in Oxford, was a teacher and established some of the first free schools in New Jersey. During the Civil War, she brought supplies to soldiers and nursed the wounded. After the war, she organized a systematic search for missing soldiers. Congress eventually funded what became known as the Missing Soldiers Office, making her the first woman to run a government bureau. In 1881, Barton created the American Red Cross to help victims of war and natural disaster.

Leonard Bernstein (1918–1990) was one of America's leading conductors and composers. In 1943, Bernstein made his conducting debut with the New York Philharmonic Orchestra. Fifteen years later, he became the first American director of the philharmonic and greatly increased its stature. Although Bernstein was also a composer of operas and ballets, he is best remembered for his scores to the musicals *West Side Story* and *On the Town*. Bernstein was born in Lawrence.

Patricia Bradley (1951–   ), a native of Westford, is the only golfer to win all four major women's championships. Bradley joined the Ladies Professional Golf Association (LPGA) tour in 1974. Since then, she has twice been named Player of the Year and has won more than 30 titles. Bradley was the first female golfer to pass $3 million in career earnings. She is a member of the LPGA Hall of Fame.

Patricia Bradley

Anne Bradstreet (1612?–1672) was the first important American poet. She was born in Northampton, England, and moved to the Massachusetts Bay Colony in 1630. Her collection *The Tenth Muse Lately Sprung Up in America*, the first book of poetry written in the American colonies, was published in 1650. Her best poems dealt with the difficult life of the settlers.

Edward Brooke

Edward Brooke (1919–) was the first African-American U.S. senator after Reconstruction, the period immediately following the Civil War. Brooke, who grew up in Washington, D.C., attended Boston University Law School. In 1962, he was elected attorney general of Massachusetts. As attorney general, he made nationwide headlines for exposing corruption in the state government. In 1966, Brooke, a Republican, was elected to U.S. Senate, becoming the first black ever elected to the Senate by a popular vote.

Bette Davis (1908–1989), one of America's greatest movie actresses, was born in Lowell. She made her film debut in 1931 in *Bad Sister* and became a star in 1934 after playing a scheming waitress in *Of Human Bondage*. Davis often appeared in melodramatic movies, playing willfully independent, intense, and eccentric characters. Her most famous films include *The Little Foxes* and *All about Eve*. Davis eventually earned ten Academy Award nominations, more than any other actress of her time, and won twice.

Geena Davis (1957–) is a popular actress, known for playing amiable, funny, and offbeat characters. Her most famous role was in *Thelma and*

Louise, in which she played one of two women who leave their humdrum lives behind as they are chased across America by the police. Davis won an Academy Award for Best Supporting Actress for her performance as a dog trainer in *The Accidental Tourist*. She was born in Wareham.

Ralph Waldo Emerson (1803–1882), a philosopher who led the transcendentalist movement, was born in Boston. His first book, *Nature*, explained the ideas behind transcendentalism, arguing for individual freedom and the view that spiritual experiences were superior to formal religion. Emerson was also active in the antislavery movement.

Fannie Farmer (1857–1915), a Boston native, was the first cook to use standard measurements in recipes. She directed the Boston Cooking School for ten years and then founded Miss Farmer's School of Cookery, where the students were housewives rather than professional cooks. She wrote the first *Fannie Farmer Cookbook* in 1896.

Fannie Farmer

William Lloyd Garrison (1805–1879), of Newburyport, was a leading antislavery activist. He published the influential antislavery newspaper the *Liberator* and helped found the American Anti-Slavery Society, serving as its president for more than 20 years. His speeches against slavery aroused great hatred in the South, and he received many death threats. Garrison also worked for women's rights, for the rights of Native Americans, and for peace.

Robert Goddard (1882–1945) was a rocket scientist whose work lay the foundation for space exploration. As a child in Worcester, Goddard dreamed of sending rockets to the moon and even to Mars at a time when no one else considered it possible. In 1926, he launched the first rocket using liquid fuel, and three years later he sent up the first rocket carrying instruments, such as a thermometer and a camera. Over the course of his career, he earned more than 200 patents related to rocketry.

Robert Goddard

Nathaniel Hawthorne (1804–1864) was one of the greatest 19th-century American writers. Hawthorne was born in Salem, and much of his work criticizes the intolerance of his Puritan ancestors. His best-known novel, *The Scarlet Letter*, concerns a woman condemned by Puritan society because she has a baby and refuses to name the father. His other books, such as *The House of the Seven Gables* and *Twice-Told Tales*, also confront ethical questions and the dark side of human nature.

Winslow Homer (1836–1910), of Boston, was an artist famous for his dramatic seascapes. Homer began his career as an illustrator for *Harper's Weekly* magazine. He later became known for his powerfully realistic paintings of nature.

John F. Kennedy (1917–1963), the youngest person ever elected president, was born in Brookline. Kennedy, a member of a prominent Massachusetts family, served as a U.S. representative and senator before being elected the nation's first Roman Catholic president. As president, he worked on civil rights legislation and promoted space exploration. He also backed an unsuccessful invasion of

John F. Kennedy

Cuba to overthrow its leader Fidel Castro. Kennedy's youth and charisma gave the nation hope, and his assassination in 1963 shocked the world.

Jack Lemmon (1925–   ), a native of Boston, is an actor who has made a career playing worried, well-meaning men in a heartless world. After working on stage and in television, he made his film debut in 1954 in *It Should Happen to You*. The following year he won a Best Supporting Actor Oscar for *Mister Roberts*. His most famous films include *Some Like It Hot*, *The Apartment*, and *The Odd Couple*. Lemmon has been nominated for eight Academy Awards.

Horace Mann (1796–1859), who was born in Franklin, is considered the father of American public education because he led the fight for free mandatory schools in the United States. As a member of the Massachusetts legislature, Mann helped establish the nation's first state board of education. After he was appointed secretary of the board of education, he became the leading figure in promoting nonreligious public education, rallying public support for increasing teachers' pay and founding schools for training teachers.

Rocky Marciano (1923–1969), of Brockton, was the only undefeated heavyweight champion in boxing history. He began boxing while serving in the U.S. Army during World War II. Marciano became heavyweight champion in 1952. By the time he retired in 1956, he had a record of 49–0 with 43 knockouts. Marciano is considered one of the hardest punchers in boxing history.

Rocky Marciano

Massasoit (1580–1661) was a Wampanoag Indian who befriended the Pilgrims. In 1621, Massasoit made a peace treaty with the Pilgrims, which lasted throughout his life. In thanks, the Pilgrims invited him and other Wampanoags to a feast which was the first Thanksgiving.

Sylvia Plath (1932–1963) was a poet and novelist from Boston whose troubled life was the source of many of her most moving works. Many of her best poems, which appear in a collection called *Ariel*, were written shortly before her suicide. They often display an obsession with self-destruction. Plath's novel *The Bell Jar* is a classic account of a young woman's breakdown.

Dr. Seuss (1904–1991), one of the world's most beloved children's authors, was born Theodor Seuss Geisel in Springfield. His richly imaginative stories are filled with outlandish creatures and clever rhymes. Dr. Seuss's classic books include *The Cat in the Hat*, *Horton Hears a Who*, *How the Grinch Stole Christmas*, and *Green Eggs and Ham*.

Dr. Seuss

Squanto (1585?–1622) was a Patuxet Indian who helped the Pilgrims survive by teaching them how to farm, fish, and hunt in Massachusetts. Before the Pilgrims arrived in America, Squanto had been kidnapped by Englishmen and sold as a slave in Spain. He eventually escaped and made his way back to America in 1619. Squanto had learned English, so in addition to teaching the Pilgrims survival skills, he also served as an interpreter.

Barbara Walters (1931–) is a television journalist famous for her frank interviews with celebrities. Walters, who was born in Boston, began her television career as a producer. In 1961, she became a reporter for NBC's *Today* show, and in 1974, she became the program's cohost. Two years later, she was lured to ABC with a $1 million contract, a record at the time.

TOUR THE STATE

Charlestown Navy Yard (Boston) The prize of the navy yard is the USS *Constitution*, which was built in 1794 and is the world's oldest warship that is still afloat. You can visit the ship's top deck and a museum filled with information about the ship's history.

Children's Museum (Boston) A gigantic bottle of milk lets you know that you've reached one of Boston's most fun-filled sites. The museum's hands-on exhibits range from Grandmother's Attic, which has old-fashioned clothes you can try on, to video cameras you can use.

Isabella Stewart Gardner Museum (Boston) One of the nation's best art museums, it is filled with such treasures as Renaissance paintings and entire rooms from European mansions.

John F. Kennedy Library (Boston) This museum has exhibits and videos about the late president and the rise of the Kennedy family. Some of Kennedy's possessions are also on display.

Museum of Science (Boston) With its talking transparent person, machine that makes lightning bolts, and state-of-the-art planetarium, this museum never lets anyone get bored.

Paul Revere House (Boston) This is the only 17th-century building still standing in Boston. The interior reflects how it looked when Paul Revere lived in it, from 1770 to 1800. Exhibits show some of Revere's possessions and silverwork.

African Meeting House (Boston) Built in 1806, this simple building is the oldest surviving African-American church in the country.

New England Aquarium (Boston) Get a close-up view of hundreds of fish, along with some playful dolphins, sea lions, and other creatures at this waterfront aquarium.

Walden Pond (Concord) Writer Henry David Thoreau made this pond famous after living alone there for two years. Today, the crush of visitors makes Thoreau's peace and solitude hard to find, but the pond is still beautiful, and you can visit a replica of Thoreau's cabin and learn about his stay.

Salem Witch Museum (Salem) A sound and light show brings the strange doings of the Salem witch hunt to life.

Cape Cod National Seashore (Eastham) Bikers, hikers, and sunbathers enjoy thousands of acres of dunes, beaches, marshes, and woods that stretch along Cape Cod.

Whaling Museum (Nantucket) Housed in an 1846 building that was originally a candle factory, this fascinating museum is filled with whaling artifacts, such as harpoons, a gigantic oil press, and a fabulous collection of items carved from baleen.

Basketball Hall of Fame (Springfield) You'll get the whole story of basketball at this museum, from its origins, when Springfield's James Naismith first threw a soccer ball into a peach basket, to stories about the game's greatest players.

Hancock Shaker Village (Pittsfield) This museum preserves 20 buildings built by the Shakers, a religious group famed for their simple, elegant, and practical crafts and buildings. The village's highlight is a round stone barn, where one man standing in the center could feed 54 cows at once.

Hancock Shaker Village

Mohawk Trail (Greenfield) This 63-mile road offers fantastic mountain vistas, quaint villages, and some of the most spectacular autumn colors found anywhere.

Mayflower II (Plymouth) This full-size replica of the ship that brought the Pilgrims to America is just 104 feet long. Costumed guides tell visitors about the cramped and stormy voyage.

Plimoth Plantation (Plymouth) Step back in time to 1627 at this re-creation of a Pilgrim village. Actors dressed in authentic costumes and speaking with 17th-century English accents go through the motions of daily life, shearing sheep, playing games, building houses, and conducting trials.

Pilgrim Monument (Provincetown) This 250-foot-tall monument marks the spot where the Pilgrims first landed in America. An observation deck at the top provides a stunning view of the tip of Cape Cod.

Southwick's Wild Animal Farm (Mendon) This farm has the largest collection of animals in New England, including rhinoceroses, camels, zebras, and giant tortoises. At the petting zoo, you can say hello to llamas, deer, and farm animals.

Old Sturbridge Village (Sturbridge) Forty buildings from around New England have been moved to this 200-acre park to re-create an early 19th-century village. Demonstrations by artisans abound, including blacksmithing, printing, and barrel making. You can even see shoes being made in the shoe shop.

FUN FACTS

Massachusetts is the site of much sports history. Basketball was invented in Springfield in 1891 by James Naismith, a physical education teacher who wanted an indoor sport for his students to play in the winter. Four years later, a YMCA director named William Morgan developed the sport of volleyball in Holyoke. And baseball's first World Series was held in Boston in 1903.

Few cities can boast as many firsts as Boston. In 1634, Boston Common became the first public park in the American colonies. The following year, the first American secondary school, Boston Latin School, opened its doors. In 1639, Boston established both the colonies' first post office and the first free public school. And in 1653, the first American public library was founded in Boston. The firsts continued during the coming years, as Boston became the site of the first newspaper published in the colonies, the first American lighthouse, and the first American subway system.

FIND OUT MORE

There's lots more to learn about Massachusetts—and your local library is a good place to start. Here are a few titles of books and videotapes that might interest you.

BOOKS

General State Books

Thompson, Kathleen. *Massachusetts*. Austin, TX: Raintree Steck-Vaughn, 1996.

Warner, J. F. *Hello U.S.A.: Massachusetts*. Minneapolis: Lerner, 1994.

Special Interest Books

Bullard, Pamela, and Judith Stoia. *The Hardest Lesson: Personal Accounts of a School Desegregation Crisis*. Boston: Little, Brown, 1980.

Cox, Clinton. *Undying Glory: The Story of the Mass. 54th Regiment*. New York: Scholastic, 1991.

Derderian, Tom. *The Boston Marathon*. Champaign, IL: Human Kinetics, 1994.

Forbes, Ester. *Johnny Tremain*. Cutchogue, NY: Buccaneer Books, 1976.

Kavanagh, Jack. *Sports Great Larry Bird*. Hillside, NJ: Enslow Publishers, 1992.

Osborne, Mary Pope. *The Many Lives of Benjamin Franklin*. New York: Dial Books, 1990.

Thayer, Bonita E. *Emily Dickinson*. New York: Franklin Watts, 1989.

Zeinert, Karen. *The Salem Witchcraft Trials*. New York: Franklin Watts, 1989.

VIDEOS AND CASSETTES

The Scarlet Letter. Washington, DC: PBS Video, 1980.

Thoreau, Henry David. *Cape Cod*. Sound recording. Ashland, OR: Classics on Tape, 1990.

Three Sovereigns for Sarah. Night Owl Productions, Alexandria, VA: PBS Video, 1990.

WEBSITES

www.state.ma.us The official website of Massachusetts is chock-full of statistics and history.

www.media3.net/plymouth All about Plymouth, where Massachusetts's first European settlers lived.

www.bostonmagazine.com A magazine with articles about city and state culture, politics, and living.

INDEX

Page numbers for charts, graphs, and illustrations are in boldface.